# Casino Secrets

**Other Huntington Press titles:**

*Bargain City: Booking, Betting, and Beating the New Las Vegas*
    by Anthony Curtis

*Comp City: A Guide to Free Las Vegas Vacations*
    by Max Rubin

*The Las Vegas Advisor Guide to Slot Clubs*
    by Jeffrey Compton

*The Theory of Blackjack: The Compleat Card Counter's Guide to the Casino Game of 21, 5th Edition*
    by Peter Griffin

*Extra Stuff: Gambling Ramblings*
    by Peter Griffin

# Casino Secrets

## Barney Vinson

### Edited by David P. Tarino

HUNTINGTON PRESS

Las Vegas, Nevada

**Casino Secrets**

Published by
   Huntington Press
   3687 South Procyon Avenue
   Las Vegas, Nevada 89103
   (702) 252-0655 Phone
   (702) 252-0675 Fax
   e-mail: lva@vegas.infi.net

**ISBN** 0-929712-02-1

Library of Congress Catalog Card Number: 96-79030

Cover Photos: Jason Cox
Cover Design: Ed Foster
Production: Jason Cox
Illustrations & Interior Design: Bethany Coffey

Safe on cover courtesy of Liberty Lock and Safe, Las Vegas
Casino on cover courtesy of Flamingo Hilton
Casino on back cover courtesy of Caesars Palace

Printing History
1st Edition—January 1997
Reprinted February 1997, May 1998

*I dedicate this book to Evelyn Brown and her daughter Debbie. Evelyn's my mother-in-law, and — well, I guess you know now who Debbie is.*

# Acknowledgments

I got a lot of help writing this book. Thanks go to Anthony Curtis and Deke Castleman of Huntington Press, who took a lump of clay and molded it into this book. My sincere appreciation and gratitude also go to David P. Tarino, without whose ideas and encouragement this book never would have happened. (I just wanted to lie on the couch and watch television, but David wouldn't let me.) Thanks also to Andrea De Witte, Phil Cooper, Rick Fields, Ed Seldney, Lenny Frome, Terry Nosek, Rich Crapis, Howard Schwartz, the Fireman, Dave Krzyzpolski, Terry Lindberg, and Ira David Sternberg for their kind assistance.

# Table of Contents

# Introduction

Your plane has just touched down in Las Vegas. There's a jumbled rush for the exit and you give the stewardess a lame smile as you follow the others out the door. You've spent a year saving up for this holiday and you want it to be perfect in every way. Who can blame you? It's expensive to travel, and there's nothing wrong with wanting to get the most from every vacation dollar you spend. You want to eat good meals, you want to see the best shows you can afford, and most of all you want to get the best gamble for your money.

I understand that, and I intend to help you do it. I've lived in Las Vegas since 1967, and over the years I've worked my way up from break-in dealer at a small casino downtown to gaming instructor at Caesars Palace on the Las Vegas Strip.

Actually, I didn't come to Las Vegas to become a dealer. I wanted to be a waiter. I figured everyone tips when they eat, so I'd have some cash in my pocket. Besides, if I worked in a restaurant I knew I wouldn't starve.

When I got to town I signed up at the Culinary Union. The first place they sent me was the Frontier Hotel, where a new gourmet restaurant was opening. Three men sat behind a table, interviewing each applicant. My turn came and I approached the men nervously, knowing how a prison inmate must feel when he goes before the parole board.

"Where have you worked?" one of the men asked me.

"Oh, different restaurants around Texas," I lied brilliantly.

"What kind of restaurants?"

"All kinds." Hey, this was easy.

"Can you flambé?"

Flambé? I was stuck. All I could do was stand there with a blank expression on my face. Needless to say, I didn't get the job, but that was probably the best thing that ever happened to me. You see, that night I walked through a Las Vegas casino and my life was changed forever. Everyone was gambling and all the dealers had money in their shirt pockets. They were getting tips — lots of tips!

Meanwhile, my life savings was down to $300. I needed a job and I needed one fast. After seeing how much money casino dealers made (or how much I thought they made, anyway), I decided that dealing was where my future lay. Most of the action seemed to be taking place at the dice tables, so I would become a crap dealer.

The decision made, I put on my best sport coat and headed for Caesars Palace. The most beautiful casino on the Strip, it attracted me like a shining beacon. Once inside, I approached a woman at the front desk. "I would like to see the person in charge," I said.

"The person in charge of what?"

"Everything."

"You mean the president?"

"Yeah, I guess so."

As she picked up the telephone, she studied me quietly. "May I have your name, please?"

"Barney Vinson, from Texas."

After a brief conversation on the phone, she directed

me to the executive offices on the third floor. I was escorted into a plush office. There was the president, having lunch with another man who was introduced to me as the hotel's entertainment director.

"What can I do for you?" the president asked me.

"I'm looking for a job."

A short pause, then: "What kind of job?"

"I don't know. I was thinking about being a crap dealer."

"Where are you working now?"

"Well, actually I'm not working right now. I just got here from Texas."

Another pause. "Have you ever worked in a casino before?"

"No sir."

Well, this went on a while longer, but why embarrass myself further? It seemed that the president of Caesars Palace thought I was some big muckety-muck gambler from Texas, and I turned out to be a country bumpkin who thought he could get a job just by applying for one. The president did take the time to kindly explain how a person got into the gaming business—first by going to school, and then starting in a small casino downtown. The example he used was professional baseball. "You start in the minor leagues (downtown)," he said, "and you work your way up to the major leagues (the Strip)."

So the next day I enrolled at a Las Vegas dealer school on Fremont Street. The tuition to learn craps was $175, which sent my life savings spiraling into the red zone. The owner of the school was a crotchety old bird named Arnold, and as soon as I forked over my money he disappeared out the door with it. Later I learned that every time he took on new students, he "invested" their tuition at a nearby casino.

Going to dealer school was not what the term implied. We didn't have assignments or homework. We didn't get diplomas. All we received for our $175 was a mimeographed sheet of paper with all the different pay-offs printed on it, and we practiced on an old dice table that was set up in the school's back room. One student would be the stickman, two others dealt the game, and the rest of us crowded around the table and made all kinds of screwball bets—just like real players do.

A couple of weeks went by and I got to the point where I could actually pay a few bets without starting a fistfight. Arnold said I was ready for the big time. That day I began looking for a job and before the end of the week I was hired at the Pioneer Club. It didn't pay much ($11 a day and free soft drinks at the snack bar), but the important thing was that I was working. At the time, the Pioneer Club was one of the more famous casinos down-town. A huge automated neon cowboy named Vegas Vic towered in front of the place. He would wave his big fiberglass hand and every half-minute or so bellow out, "Howdy Pardnuh." Vic made just enough racket to chase most people away. Still, the Pioneer Club was one of downtown's greatest landmarks, and here I was work-ing there.

I guess I should explain exactly what my job was, because it certainly had to be explained to me. I was a shill and a break-in dealer. As a shill, I stood at the dice table and acted like I was playing in order to lure real players to the game. I was sort of like a worm on a fish-ing hook. For some reason, most people don't like to gamble by themselves, so if they thought I was gambling then they would gamble, too. When the game filled up with players, I got to take a break. Sometimes, if the boss was in a good mood, he would let me take one of the regular dealers off the game, hence the rest of my job description: break-in dealer. As soon as I made a mis-take, off the table I went. Consequently, I rarely got a chance to deal for more than 15 seconds.

The only bright spot was filling up with free drinks

at the snack bar. Unfortunately, that didn't last long. Somebody hit a keno ticket for $1,500 and the casino retaliated by taking the free drinks away from the employees. It was time to move on.

In downtown Las Vegas, summer was the season when tourism reached its zenith. If you wanted a better job, summer was the time to pester the casinos, and the greener you were, the better your chances of getting hired. The casinos figured that beginners could barely keep out of their own way. They were more likely to do as they were told. Break-ins didn't know how to hustle players for tips, which was taboo, and they worked cheap.

The word on the street was that the Mint was hiring. The Mint isn't around anymore, but back in the late '60s it was the top casino downtown. It was owned by millionaire Del Webb, who also owned the Sahara Hotel and a piece of the New York Yankees baseball team. Comparing the Mint with the Pioneer was like comparing the Taj Mahal with the Leaning Tower of Pisa. "Oh please, God," I prayed, "let me go to work at the Mint and I'll never ask You for another favor again."

I approached the pit boss at the Mint. "I'm looking for a job dealing craps," I said. I was getting better at this all the time.

"Oh? Where are you working now?"

"The Pioneer."

"When can you start?"

"Today."

Bingo! I was in. My pay took a giant leap upwards: from $11 a day to $15 a day, and every day I got a *free meal!* I still wasn't a dealer by any stretch of the imagination, but I was now officially a "student" dealer, which meant I got to eat real food and practice on a real table with real dealers.

After three months of this, I was finally assigned to a regular dice crew. The first night I made $72 in tips and suddenly my life was in perfect balance with nature—

not to mention the finance company that was about to repossess my Ford Mustang.

Working at the Mint was a lot like being in the military. The camaraderie with the other dealers on my crew was unlike any other that I ever experienced. We went into battle together eight hours a day, the four of us risking life and limb against the customers. And the bosses.

This was back before civil rights and equal rights. If one of the bosses didn't like you, you were out on your ear, simple as that. You kept your head down and you didn't talk back, and if you were assigned to do a "double" you did it without complaining. A double is two eight-hour shifts back to back ... 16 hours at a stretch ... and you planned on doing one every Saturday, which was the busiest day of the week.

Some of the dealers got through those double shifts by having a drink or two on their hourly breaks. All you had to do was leave your casino and go into the one next door. The bartenders there kept the drinks coming as long as there was money on the counter. It wasn't unusual at about the ten-hour point to see dealers begin to drop like flies. One minute a dealer would be paying bets; the next he would be lying on the floor with a blank look on his face. The funny part of it was that most of the bosses thought the dealers were passing out because they were overworked.

The Mint's big boss, the boss the other bosses answered to, was named Angel. Angel terrified everybody. He was an ex-boxer and ex-security guard, and could say more with one cold stare than anyone I ever met in my life. With Angel around, you didn't need bouncers or policemen, or even the United States Army for that matter. Angel took care of everything. If there was an argument at one of the games, Angel decided it. If a fight broke out, Angel finished it. If a dealer got sick and wanted to go home, the worst possible words he could hear were, "Go see Angel."

One day an ashen-faced dealer was sent to see this boss of bosses. "I can't finish the shift," he groaned. "I'm sick."

"Waddaya mean, you're sick?"

"I'm sick. I've got this sharp pain in my stomach and I feel like I'm going to pass out."

Angel studied the dealer closely. "You're not sick," he finally announced, as if he were a doctor at the Mayo Clinic and not just a shift boss at some sawdust gambling joint. Then he clapped the dealer on the shoulder. "Now get back to work."

That night the dealer wound up in the emergency room at a Las Vegas hospital, suffering from a ruptured appendix. The only reason he didn't die was because his roommate came home and found him unconscious on the couch. I know. That dealer on the couch was me!

In May 1969, I applied for a job at a dazzling new resort due to open near the Las Vegas Strip. As I filled out my application at the Landmark, I remember saying to myself, "Oh please, God, let me get this job and I'll never ask You for another favor again." My prayer was answered and I was notified to report for pre-opening indoctrination the following month.

The Landmark was slated to open July 2, 1969. Inspired by Seattle's Space Needle, it stood across the street from Kirk Kerkorian's new International (now the Las Vegas Hilton). Actually, the Landmark had stood there since 1961, and the fact that it took almost a decade to get the doors open should have made me a bit suspicious about going to work there. But the Landmark was so different from anything else in Las Vegas that I figured it would become one of the most popular casinos in town, and consequently I would become wealthy beyond my wildest dreams.

So the proud moment arrived, and finally, after all those years, the doors of the Landmark were thrown open for the first time. Sleek limousines and fancy cars lined up along the curving entranceway, and I was there—in a crisp white shirt—ready for the big time. Oh, it was great. For about two days, that is, until I realized that the Landmark was a big fat dud.

First of all, it was competing with the International, which had Barbra Streisand in the showroom and 2,000 guest rooms. The Landmark was tiny by comparison. There was a casino on the ground floor and a smaller casino on the top floor, and the only way to get from one to the other was by taking one of four slow-moving elevators. I was working on the top floor. When my 20-minute lunch break came, it took me five minutes to get downstairs to the restaurant, five minutes to get my food, and five minutes to get back upstairs to the casino. Needless to say, I didn't have time to eat very much, but it didn't matter—I lost my appetite when I got my first day's tips. I made $20, and the next day I didn't make anything at all.

I stuck it out for almost two weeks, but it was hard. The weather was nice that summer, and my gleaming motorcycle (which I bought while working at the Mint) sat poised in the employee parking lot, raring to take me anywhere I wanted to go. One afternoon I wandered out to the parking lot on my break and the next thing I knew I was seated on my motorcycle smoking a cigarette. Before I realized it, I had switched on the ignition key and kicked the motor to life. Suddenly, I was tooling out of the lot and my stint at the Landmark was over. It was a foolish thing to do, but I was young.

Then came the hard realities of life. I was back where I started two years before: out of work and low on cash. It was time to pound the pavement again. That's when a friend from my days at the Mint told me about a friend of his named Bill who was working at the Dunes. The Dunes was one of the classiest resorts on the Strip, but it took an act of Congress to get a job there. Either that, or a recommendation from somebody close to the man who did the hiring, and it turned out that Bill was one of that man's best friends. It seemed as though everyone in town knew everyone else…except me.

As it turned out, Bill liked to gamble, but preferred to do so with other people's money. So Bill's friend told me that if I "lent" his friend Bill $500, Bill would in turn introduce me to *his* friend. In other words, I might get a job at the Dunes, but it was going to cost me $500. To make it even more confusing, I got most of the money together by borrowing it from Bill's friend at the Mint! "Please God," I remember whispering as I handed the money to Bill that night. "Let me get this job and I'll never ask You for another favor again."

This was my one and only experience with that famous Las Vegas aphorism known as "juice"—and a week later I was working at the Dunes. The Dunes is gone now, but at that time it was one of the most successful casinos in Vegas. It was high-roller heaven, and I never saw so many diamond rings and $100 bills in my life.

One of the hotel's owners was Major Riddle. He was a gambler and a showman. He was also the first to present bare-breasted showgirls in a Las Vegas showroom. The show, *Minsky's Follies*, prompted the local Catholic bishop to call for censorship. Everyone else called for reservations! Sixteen thousand people saw it in a single week, which set a longtime Vegas attendance record.

In those days, men loved to shoot craps. Their wives or girlfriends would play blackjack or the slot machines, and the kids stayed home. The Dunes was renowned for its junket play, with a New York group coming in every Sunday and another group from Miami or St. Louis every Wednesday. We would line up at our tables like soldiers in pill boxes, waiting for the "enemy" to charge through the front door.

It was an era when anything could happen and usually did. One night a tall young woman approached the pit boss and asked directions to the powder room. In a particularly good mood that evening, the boss said, "I'll tell you where the powder room is if you'll tell me how tall you are."

"It's none of your business," she snapped, turning on her high heels and striding away.

Five minutes later she returned. Marching up to the pit boss, she threw her dress up over her head, revealing nothing underneath! "That's how tall I am," she announced, then down came her dress and off she went.

The pit boss related this story years later, but what made it so remarkable was that not one gambler in the entire casino ever saw what happened. Everyone was so busy gambling that nothing else mattered—not even a tall young woman with her dress over her head.

One night an Asian man was playing craps. He took a marker for $10,000, but hadn't signed it yet. After losing the money, he keeled over with a heart attack and had to be rushed to the hospital. The owner of the hotel instructed one of the pit supervisors to pay the man a visit, not to see how he was doing, but to get him to sign that $10,000 marker. Otherwise, the casino would never get the money back. So the pit supervisor drove to the hospital on his day off, and spent an hour visiting with the man. He also got the man to sign the marker, which he then took back to the casino.

Well, it turned out that the Asian owned a Mercedes Benz dealership in Hong Kong. He was so grateful to the pit supervisor for visiting him in the hospital that he shipped him a brand new Mercedes Benz every year free of charge. This continued until the Asian's death, 12 years later.

I watched Las Vegas change dramatically during my years at the Dunes, and even more after I moved to Caesars Palace. In response to competition from 47 other states, Las Vegas took a hard look at its customer base.

Today the casino visitor is king. When I first moved to Las Vegas, there weren't enough casinos to go around, and no one cared if you were mistreated. Today, with 80 casinos in Vegas, this is no longer true. Each casino now stresses courtesy more than anything in order to keep its customers from going somewhere else.

The big problem facing casinos nowadays is that many novice gamblers are afraid to play the table games. The dealer might give them a dirty look or one of the players might get mad at them if they make a mistake. So they play the slot machines or nothing at all. This is the reason that some casinos have instituted free gaming lessons. Beginners can learn the basics of all the games—in a real casino atmosphere—without fear of intimidation or embarrassment. In fact, each year more than 24,000 people take complimentary gaming classes at Caesars Palace, and this is only one of a dozen casinos in Las Vegas where instructional classes are offered.

Just remember one thing. Even if you play a casino game properly, the house will usually have the edge. You can cut that edge considerably, however, by following a few basic rules. So get comfortable. You're about to learn the right way to play every popular game in the casino. Maybe you'll win enough to make it all worthwhile, or at least make buying this book worthwhile!

# 1
# Blackjack

## *The Best Game in the House*

The fundamental concept of blackjack is simple. You want to get a higher total than the dealer without going over 21. Face cards count as 10, and an ace can be counted as 1 or 11. A blackjack (also known as a "natural") is an ace and any 10 on your first two cards. It wins automatically (unless the dealer also has a blackjack, in which case it's a tie), and pays $1\frac{1}{2}$ times your bet. The game got its name because in its early days a player was paid extra if one of his first two cards was a black jack. (If more than two black jacks showed up in the deck, the player probably got hit over the *head* with a blackjack.)

Back in those days blackjack wasn't as popular as it is today. Everything changed when professor of mathematics Edward Thorp wrote a book called *Beat the Dealer*, which introduced an exciting technique known as card counting. By calculating the ratio of big cards to small cards left in the deck, a good counter found himself in the enviable position of being able to beat the casino at its own game. Suddenly everybody wanted to be a blackjack expert. The game (and the book) soared in popularity.

The potential of Thorp's system scared the casino owners to death. Thinking that they would all go bankrupt, the casinos began ejecting any player they suspected of counting cards and instituting such changes as dealing the cards from multiple-deck boxes (known as "shoes") and shuffling the cards more often. Truth is, that book on card counting was the best thing that ever happened to the game. Blackjack is now the most popular table game in the casinos, yet surveys continue to show that almost no one plays it correctly.

If you intend to gamble with your hard-earned money, you should at least play the percentages and get the house edge down to something you can live with. At blackjack, that house edge (or advantage) against most players usually falls in the range of 1%-3%, depending on your skill level.

The main reason the house has the edge at blackjack is the fact that you must make your decisions before the dealer makes his. If you go over 21 and "bust," that's the end of the hand for you. If the dealer also busts, later in the same hand, it's too late. You've already lost your money. That's why it's important to learn when to take another card and when not to. By learning what's known as blackjack's "basic strategy," you can lower the house edge to less than 1%, making it one of the best games in the casino.

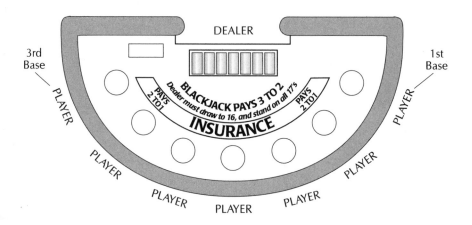

Basic strategy is a simple and proven system that doesn't require a lot of brainwork and concentration, but does take a little bit of study to memorize completely. Both an abbreviated version, as well as the complete basic strategy, are provided on pages 24 and 25. In the meantime, here's a rule of thumb that will help you: just assume that the dealer's bottom card is a 10. Why? Because there are more 10s and face cards in the deck than anything else, so chances are good that the dealer's "hole card" is a 10. For the same reason, you should assume that the next card dealt will also be a 10. Therefore, let's say you're dealt a 9 and a 7. You have a total of 16. The dealer is showing a 6. Do you want another card? No you don't, because chances are the next card is going to be a 10, and the dealer will bust instead of you.

Remember this, too: for decision-making, the dealer's up card is usually just as important as the total of your cards. Your decisions should be based not just on what you hold, but also on what the dealer has.

Experts say that nearly 40% of your starting hands will be "stiffs," or bad hands. You won't get a 19 or 20 every time. Then again, neither will the dealer. Using basic strategy, you'll win much of the time even with a bad hand—simply because the dealer must draw until he has at least 17. He's forced (by the rules) to take another card when he's got a bad hand. You are not. Once again, it's important to remember that the object is not simply to get a good hand. It's to beat the dealer.

You've probably heard that one player at the table who doesn't play properly can adversely change the outcome for everyone else. Especially the player in the last position, or the "hot seat," as it's called. The reason for this, according to legend, is that the strategy of the player in the hot seat is supposed to affect the cards that the dealer gets. This is simply not true. Granted, half the time a bad play will help the dealer, but half the time it will hurt him. So it really isn't important how anyone else at the table plays his hand. Everyone is playing his own cards against the dealer's cards.

Most gamblers, however, like to blame someone else when they lose. Who are they going to blame at the dice table? The shooter! Who are they going to blame at the blackjack game? The person sitting in the hot seat, that's who.

One fear most novice blackjack players have is that the dealer will skip them if they take too long to make a decision, or that other players at the table will get angry if they don't act quickly. If you're not sure whether you want another card or not, what will the dealer do? He'll stand there and wait, that's all. As far as the other players are concerned, remember what I said earlier. The majority of them don't know what they're doing anyway, so what do you care what they think?

Basic strategy works, so memorize it, follow it faithfully, and use it consistently. If the dealer has a bad card up (2, 3, 4, 5, or 6) and you have 12 or more in your hand, don't take another card. Make the dealer take that big card that (you hope) is coming. If the dealer has a good card up (7, 8, 9, 10, or ace) and you have 16 or less, take another card. I know we are assuming the next card is a 10, but in this case you have to take it anyway. After all, if the dealer has an 8 up, we are assuming he has 18—and if the dealer has 18 and you have 16, you lose anyway. By taking another card you at least have a chance of improving your hand against the dealer's strong card. If you lose, at least you'll lose "intelligently." (That should make you feel better.)

There is one case that defies the rule of thumb. It's when you have 12 and the dealer shows a 2 or 3. Rather than standing in anticipation of the dealer breaking, you should go ahead and hit your 12.

Never hit a hard 17. You've got to stop somewhere when you play blackjack, and a hard 17 (any cards that add up to 17) is the place. It doesn't matter what the dealer's up card is. Always stop at 17. In fact, the dealers in most casinos have orders that if a player wants to hit a 17, they have to stop the game and notify the pit boss. "Hitting hard 17!" the dealer will call—and suddenly you're looking for a rock to crawl under.

Always hit a soft 17. A soft 17 (ace and a 6, for example) doesn't have to be counted as 17. It's better to count it as 7 and hit (or double down against dealer low cards). Standing on a soft 17 is one of the most common and costly errors made in blackjack.

**CASINO SECRET**

If you have a hand with lots of cards and maybe an ace or two, it might get a little confusing. It's okay to show the dealer your cards and ask her to count them up for you.

Basic strategy won't give you the advantage, but the beauty of this system is that it takes all the guesswork out of the game. No longer will you have to rely on hunches or gut feelings. Every play is decided by just two things: your two cards and the dealer's up card. By making a science out of the game, you will lower the house edge to under 1%.

Now let's talk about some of the options available in a blackjack game. If you're going to war with the casino at the blackjack table, you need to be familiar with all the weapons in your arsenal.

### Splitting Pairs

If you're dealt two cards of equal value (two 8s, two 9s, etc.), you are allowed to split them and make two separate hands out of your original hand. Simply turn the cards face up and tell the dealer you want to split. You'll have to match your original bet with an equal bet on the second hand. The two hands are then played out independently of one another.

When to split and when not to is spelled out in the basic strategy. In general, you will split more often when the dealer has a low card up. You certainly don't want to split 7s if the dealer is showing a 10, for example. On the other hand, if the dealer is showing a 2-7, splitting 7s is definitely worthwhile.

**Always split aces.** The reason you split aces is obvious. There are a lot of cards that will combine with an ace to give you a good hand. The casino retaliates by allowing you only one card on each ace. Don't worry. It's still worth it. Split aces regardless of the dealer's up card.

**Always split 8s.** First of all, 16 is the worst hand you can get. If you draw and the next card is a 6, 7, 8, 9, or 10 you'll bust and lose your bet. By splitting 8s, you have a good chance of making two decent hands out of one bad one. Split 8s regardless of the dealer's up card.

**Never split 10s**. You already have 20, and the only thing that can beat you is 21. It doesn't make good sense, yet I still see people splitting 10s all the time.

Not long ago I saw a player bet $500. He was dealt two 10s. The dealer was showing a 6, so the player split the 10s, putting another $500 in action. He wound up with 16 on one hand and 14 on the other. Meanwhile, the dealer drew a small card and beat everyone at the table. The player who split his 10s wound up losing $1,000, whereas he would have won $500 by playing his cards properly.

If you want to get some dirty looks from the other players at the table, split 10s. I want you to set this book down right now, raise your right hand, and repeat after me, "I WILL NOT SPLIT TENS."

Thank you.

**Never split 4s or 5s.** What are you going to wind up with if you split 4s? Two 14s, that's what. And it's the same story when you split 5s. With other pairs (2s, 3s, 6s,

7s, and 9s), it depends on what the dealer is showing. If the dealer is showing a low card (4, 5, or 6), get as much money on the table as you can by splitting those pairs. If the dealer is showing a high card (7, 8, 9, 10, or ace), get out of the hand as cheaply as you can.

## Doubling Down

After seeing your original two cards, you can double your bet and take one extra card. This is an important option because, like splitting pairs, you have the chance to get more money into the game when the odds are in your favor. For example, let's say you're dealt a 7 and a 4. This adds up to 11. If your next card is a 10, you'll have a perfect 21.

**Always double down with 11.** Match your original bet and the dealer will give you one more card. Playing the percentages, you're way ahead of the game when you double down with an 11—even if the dealer has a high card showing. If you double down against a ten or ace and the dealer winds up with a blackjack, the double-down portion of your bet will be returned to you.

**Double down with 10 unless the dealer is showing a 10 or an ace.** Again, you are playing the percentages, which indicate that you don't put up additional money to buck the dealer's 10 or ace. Remember, you only want to put more money into action when you have the odds in your favor.

**Double down with an ace and 2, 3, 4, 5, 6, or 7 if the dealer is showing a 5 or 6.** This is called a soft double down. You're hoping the dealer will break with his weak up card. But even if he doesn't, you still have a chance to make a good hand of your own. (Note: Some casinos will only allow you to double down with 10 or 11. Don't play there if you have a choice.)

## Insurance

If the dealer's up card is an ace, he will offer you a chance to take "insurance." You can take insurance for any amount up to half your original bet. Don't stack it on top of your bet. Instead, place this additional money inside the insurance box on the table.

The dealer will then check his bottom card to see if he has a blackjack. If he does, you lose your original bet (unless you also have a blackjack), but get paid 2-1 for your insurance bet (which makes the whole transaction a wash). If the dealer does not have a blackjack, you lose your insurance bet and the hand continues.

All experts agree on one thing. *Insurance is not recommended.* If the dealer is showing an ace, he will probably wind up with a very good hand and you risk losing your original wager plus the extra insurance bet.

The only time I consider taking insurance is when I have a blackjack of my own. If you have a natural, you can call for "even money." It's the same thing as taking insurance, only you don't have to put more money on the table and the dealer doesn't even check to see if he has a blackjack. By taking even money, you get paid whether the dealer has a blackjack or not. It's a sure winner. The problem is you give up the 3-2 bonus payoff.

From a purely mathematical point of view, you should never take insurance—even when you have a blackjack of your own. So when the dealer flips over that ace and says "insurance" in a friendly voice, just pretend you didn't hear him.

## Surrender

Many casinos now offer an option called "surrender." If you are not happy with your first two cards and the dealer doesn't have a blackjack, you're allowed to surrender. This means you give up half your original bet to get out of the hand.

A lot of people who play blackjack think this is one

of the greatest innovations since J. Edgar Hoover invented the vacuum cleaner, and subsequently get carried away and overuse the option. Ask yourself this question: How much money can you win if you give up half your bet and drop out of the hand? As long as you're in the game, you have a chance of winning. If you surrender, you have no chance at all. Basic strategy tells us to surrender 15 against a dealer ten and 16 (except a pair of 8s) against a dealer ten or ace. That's all.

## Etiquette

A small sign on each table tells you what the minimum and maximum bets are on that game. Don't do as I did when I first came to Las Vegas. I tossed a $20 bill on the table and asked for change. The game came to a complete stop while the dealer counted out my chips. Then I realized to my dismay that it was a $25 table.

Never place cameras, purses, or other personal possessions on the table. Don't put them on the floor, either. There are a lot of people walking around with very sticky fingers.

For security reasons, many casinos deal the player's cards face up. If so, never touch the cards. Use hand signals to indicate that you want to hit or stand. These are the three hand signals you should know:

• If you want another card, make a scratching motion on the table with your finger.
• If you don't want another card, move your hand sideways behind your bet.
• If you get a card you don't like, ball your hand into a fist and pound it on the table.

If you split pairs or double down, place your additional bet next to your original wager. Never stack the money when making additional bets; place it alongside your original wager.

In games where the cards are dealt face down, you are allowed to handle them, but be sure to use only one hand. The dealer will scold you if you use two hands to hold the cards. Scratch the cards gently on the felt to request a hit. Tuck the cards underneath your bet to indicate that you want to stand. Don't pick up your chips to put your cards beneath them. Casinos don't like customers touching unresolved bets. By gently sliding your cards on the felt, you'll find that the cards slip easily under the chips.

In these face-down games, it's up to you to keep track of the total of your hand. I once sat next to a player who spoke no English. I could see that his first two cards were a 10 and a 3. He drew and received a 9 for a busting total of 22. It didn't matter. The man signaled for another hit and drew an ace. He drew again and got a 2. Again, ace. Again, another 2. Now, I could see that the man had 28, but the dealer could only see 18 on the layout. When the man signaled for another hit, the dealer cautiously delivered a 9 for 37 total and 27 on the board. The man was laughing and motioning to hit again as the dealer struggled to pry the cards out of his hands. I think the man thought the object of the game was to get more cards than the other players at the table. When you bust, it's up to you to let the dealer know. Simply turn all of your cards face up and the dealer will collect them.

You must also turn your cards up right away when you get a natural. You'll get paid at the rate of 3-2 unless the dealer also has a natural.

After the dealer shuffles the cards, he may offer you a plastic "cut" card. Don't jump back when he does this. He's merely asking you cut the cards. Place the card into the deck at any point. The dealer will then cut the cards at that spot, and insert the cut card somewhere toward the back of the deck. When he reaches the cut card during the game, he will finish the hand and reshuffle the cards.

Before dealing the first hand, the dealer will "burn" a card. The first card from the shoe is placed face down in the discard rack. This doesn't affect anything; it's just tradition.

Most dealers rely on tips to make a living. Whatever the minimum wage is, that's usually what a dealer earns. So if the dealer has been pleasant and helpful, you might want to express your appreciation by tipping. You can either give the dealer a direct tip, or you can make a bet for him. A dealer's bet goes just in front of your bet on the table. When you win, the dealer wins. If you lose, so does the dealer.

Remember, gambling is supposed to be fun, so play blackjack with the idea that, while you might lose, you'll have some fun doing it. It is much more thrilling to match wits against another human than it is to play a slot machine. There's also the idea that anything can happen on a "live" game, as the following story illustrates.

A young man sat down at a blackjack table. He played for 45 minutes, betting $5 per hand, and he never lost! A well-dressed man was standing behind the table, watching the young man play. Finally, he asked the young man timidly, "Would you mind if I made a bet on your next hand?"

The young man shrugged. "I don't care."

The well-dressed man reached into his pocket, took out $2,000 in cash, and placed it on top of the young man's $5 bet.

The dealer dealt the young man two 10s. The young man turned to the man behind him and said, "If you don't give me $500, I'm going to hit that 20!"

# Complete Basic Strategy for Single and Multiple Deck Blackjack

## Hit-Stand

|    | 2 | 3 | 4 | 5 | 6 | 7 | 8 | 9 | T | A |
|----|---|---|---|---|---|---|---|---|---|---|
| 12 | H | H | S | S | S | H | H | H | H | H |
| 13 | S | S | S | S | S | H | H | H | H | H |
| 14 | S | S | S | S | S | H | H | H | H | H |
| 15 | S | S | S | S | S | H | H | H | H | H |
| 16 | S | S | S | S | S | H | H | H | H | H |
| 17 | S | S | S | S | S | S | S | S | S | S |

## Hard Double

|    | 2 | 3 | 4 | 5 | 6 | 7 | 8 | 9 | T | A |
|----|---|---|---|---|---|---|---|---|---|---|
| 11 | D | D | D | D | D | D | D | D | D | D/H |
| 10 | D | D | D | D | D | D | D | D | H | H |
| 9  | D/H | D | D | D | D | H | H | H | H | H |
| 8  | H | H | H | D/H | D/H | H | H | H | H | H |

## Soft Double

|    | 2 | 3 | 4 | 5 | 6 | 7 | 8 | 9 | T | A |
|----|---|---|---|---|---|---|---|---|---|---|
| A9 | .......................... ALWAYS STAND .......................... |||||||||| 
| A8 | S | S | S | S | D/S | S | S | S | S | S |
| A7 | S | D | D | D | D | S | S | H | H | S*/H |
| A6 | D/H | D | D | D | D | H | H | H | H | H |
| A5 | H | H | D | D | D | H | H | H | H | H |
| A4 | H | H | D | D | D | H | H | H | H | H |
| A3 | H | H | D/H | D | D | H | H | H | H | H |
| A2 | H | H | D/H | D | D | H | H | H | H | H |

## Split Pairs

|    | 2 | 3 | 4 | 5 | 6 | 7 | 8 | 9 | T | A |
|----|---|---|---|---|---|---|---|---|---|---|
| 22 | H | P/H | P | P | P | P | H | H | H | H |
| 33 | H | H | P | P | P | P | H | H | H | H |
| 44 | ........................... NEVER SPLIT .......................... |||||||||| 
| 55 | ........................... NEVER SPLIT .......................... |||||||||| 
| 66 | P/H | P | P | P | P | H | H | H | H | H |
| 77 | P | P | P | P | P | P | H | H | S/H | H |
| 88 | ........................... ALWAYS SPLIT .......................... |||||||||| 
| 99 | P | P | P | P | P | S | P | P | S | S |
| TT | ........................... NEVER SPLIT .......................... |||||||||| 
| AA | ........................... ALWAYS SPLIT .......................... |||||||||| 

NEVER TAKE INSURANCE

\* Hit (A,7) vs. ace if dealer hits soft 17.

KEY:  H= Hit    S=Stand    P=Split Pair    D=Double Down

## How to Use Complete Basic Strategy Chart
## (previous page)

The combinations down the left hand side of the chart represent your hand. The numbers across the top represent the dealer's up card. Example: You hold (A,4) and the dealer shows a 6, the proper play is to double down. Where there is a slash (i.e., D/H), the first play is versus a single deck and the second is versus multiple decks. The most important tables are Hit-Stand and Hard Double. They are also easiest to learn.

### Abbreviated Basic Strategy

1) Always split eights and aces.
2) Double 10 and 11 against dealer's 2-9.
3) You hold 12-16; dealer shows 2-6—stand.
4) You hold 12-16; dealer shows 7, 8, 9, T, A—hit.
5) Stand on 17-21, except always hit on soft 17.
6) Never take insurance.

# Multi-Action Blackjack

Available in some casinos, Multi-Action blackjack is a version of the game that gives you three times the action for your money. What you're doing is playing three rounds of blackjack in a single hand against the dealer's single up card. Each round is the same as one complete hand in regular blackjack, and you still have all the options of regular blackjack.

After you play your hands, the dealer plays his by drawing one or more cards. He then pays or takes all first-round wagers.

The dealer then discards his hit cards, leaving his original up card on the layout. Now he completes his hand again and pays or picks up second-round bets.

The dealer discards his hit cards on that hand, and plays his hand a third time. Then he pays or takes all third round wagers and a new series of play begins.

In Multi-Action blackjack, you must play at least two of the three hands. You can double down and surrender on one or more hands, but if you split pairs you must double your bets on all hands you play.

The drawback to Multi-Action blackjack is that when you get a bad hand and bust, you lose all three hands! A bad run of cards can hurt you good here. I recommend sticking with regular blackjack. The house percentage is the same and the risk isn't quite so great.

# Spanish 21

This is a spinoff of regular blackjack and is being loudly hailed as the next big table game in Las Vegas. Spanish 21 is played with six special 48-card decks in which the ten-spot cards have been removed. You would think that the player's chances of winning would be diminished by having all the 10s removed, and you would be right. With fewer 10-count cards in the deck, the dealer will not break as often. However, there are some generous concessions the casino offers in return, making the game much more exciting than regular blackjack.

• Player may double down on any total and any number of cards, including after splitting.
• Hitting and doubling allowed after splitting.
• Surrender.
• Double-down rescue allows player to take back double-down portion of a wager and forfeit the original wager.
• Player blackjack beats dealer blackjack and pays 3-2.
• Player 21-point total beats dealer 21-point total; otherwise all ties are pushes.
• Double down on any number of cards.
• Bonus payoffs on special hands:
> A 5-card 21 pays 3-2.
> A 6-card 21 pays double.
> A 7-card 21 pays triple.
> A 6-7-8 in mixed suits pays 3-2.
> A 6-7-8 in the same suit pays double.
> A 6-7-8 (all spades) pays triple.
> Three 7s in mixed suits pays 3-2.
> Three 7s in the same suit pays double.
> Three 7s in spades pays triple.
• There is also a Super Jackpot Bonus of $1,000 to any player who gets three suited 7s when the dealer's up card is also a 7. And when this happens, every other player in the game gets a $50 "envy" jackpot!

The house edge against the perfect basic strategy (different from the standard basic) is less than 1%. If you're going to play this novel blackjack game, here are some suggestions.

• Always hit a hard 12 or 13, no matter what the dealer's up card is.
• Don't double down with 10 against the dealer's 8, 9, 10, or ace.
• Don't double down with 11 against the dealer's 9, 10 or ace.
• Don't split 8s against a dealer ace.
• Use the double-down rescue option when you double to a stiff total and the dealer's up card is 8 through ace.
• Never take insurance (the removal of the tens makes insurance an even worse bet than in standard blackjack).

# 2
# Craps

## *Not as Scary as it Looks*

One of the most exciting games in the casino is craps. Its origins are unknown, but dice made from animal knuckles (hence the term "bones") have been uncovered in ruins dating back to biblical times. Craps was introduced to New Orleans from Europe in the middle of the 18th century, but the game didn't really become popular until World War II. That's when GIs learned to play, and the game hasn't been the same since.

The problem with craps is that most novices are intimidated by the table layout. By studying the table closely, however, you will find that both ends of the layout are the same (so it's only half as scary as it looks)— the bets in the middle of the table are long shots that you don't really need to understand, because you shouldn't be making them in the first place.

The concept of the game is simple. If you want to bet with the dice, bet on the pass line. If the shooter wins, you win. If you want to bet against the dice, bet on the don't pass. If the shooter loses, you win. (Exception: If the first roll is a 12, you don't win or lose on the don't pass. It is a push, or a "bar" roll.)

The shooter wins by rolling a 7 or 11 (these are called "naturals") on the first roll. The shooter loses by rolling craps (2, 3, or 12) on the first roll. Any other number (4,

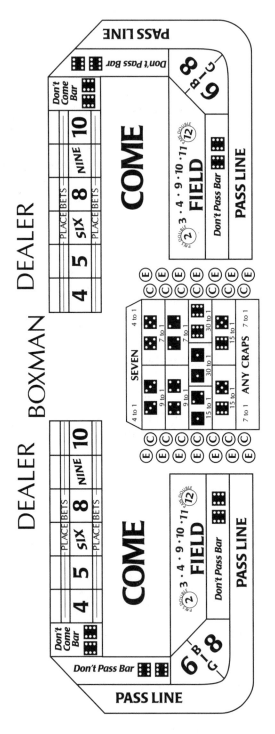

5, 6, 8, 9, or 10) becomes the shooter's point, and to win he has to roll that number again before rolling another 7.

Before you bet, make sure that it's the first roll of a sequence, called the "come-out" roll. You can tell by looking at the position of the circular disc called the "puck" (sometimes "buck"). If the puck lies white-side-up on one of the box numbers (4, 5, 6, 8, 9, 10), that number is the current point and a roll is in progress. If the puck lies black-side-up in the don't come box, it's a come-out roll and bets may be placed. Place your bet on the table directly in front of you.

The dice pass from player to player clockwise, and everyone gets a chance to shoot. You don't have to throw the dice, but most players consider this an essential part of the game. Just think, for once in your life you have some control over destiny—and besides, no one can shoot those dice as good as you can! The late Benny Binion (original owner of the Horseshoe) once said that the reason craps was so popular was because by shooting the dice it made the game "a physical thing."

There are several things to remember if you do decide to shoot. First, you must keep the dice over the table; they have to be in plain view at all times. (Don't go dancing off across the room with them.) Second, the stickman will ask you to throw the dice all the way to the other end of the table. This is to make sure the roll is fair and to avoid controversies and arguments over the way the dice were thrown.

When I was working at the Dunes, a well-heeled New Yorker was getting ready to shoot the dice at the crap table. He bet $500 on the pass line, and he spread another $2,700 in bets across the table. In those days, that was the maximum amount of money that a player could bet, so this was a big deal. I might also add that customer courtesy wasn't stressed like it is nowadays, either.

On his first roll, he lobbed the dice high in the air and they came to a stop about two feet from the other end of the table. "Hey, buddy," the floor supervisor said, looking the New Yorker dead in the eye. "You gotta shoot the dice all the way to the other end."

"I'll shoot the dice any way I want," the player replied with a smirk.

On his next roll, the New Yorker lobbed the dice even higher in the air. Again, they stopped two feet from the other end of the table.

The floor supervisor picked up all the man's chips and shoved them in front of him. "Take your money," he barked, "and get out of here!"

"You can't talk to me like that. I'm—"

"GET THE HELL OUTTA HERE!"

And that was the end of our "high roller" from New York.

Occasionally, the dice will go flying off the table. If that occurs while you're shooting, don't worry about it. It only happens about 300 times a day in each Las Vegas casino. Unfortunately, most gamblers are superstitious, and there is an old saying at the dice table that goes like this: "Dice on the floor, seven at the door." Every player at the table will usually take all his bets down, and if dirty looks could kill you'd be on your way to Arlington.

There is a way of getting out of this sticky situation, however. After throwing the dice off the table, simply say, "Same dice." That's what the pros do. You don't want to shoot with just any old dice; you want the same dice you were shooting. It's pure superstition, of course, but every seasoned dice player does it. No more dirty looks, no more worries about bombs in your luggage. Suddenly you're everyone's friend again.

And that's the beauty of this game. It's you and the others against the dice, a kinship unlike any other in the casino. Just take a look around. You will find that the dice tables are always located right in the heart of the casino. If the dice tables are cranking, there's an air of excitement that sweeps through the whole room. If the dice tables are quiet, the entire casino takes on the atmosphere of a ghost town.

In fact, if you play the game properly, the house edge at craps is less than 1%. The only other table games that compare with it are baccarat and basic strategy blackjack. So let's play craps, and let's play it the way the experts do.

### The Odds

The reason the house edge at craps is so low is because of the odds bet, which you can make once the shooter has established a point. If the shooter wins, you get paid the true amount for your odds, giving the house absolutely no advantage on that portion of the bet. The amount of odds you can take varies from casino to casino, but you are usually allowed to take at least double odds on your pass line bet. (In other words, you can bet up to double whatever your pass line bet is.) The odds are placed directly behind your original bet on the pass line.

The odds work like this. Let's say the shooter's point is 10. There are three ways to roll a 10: 5-5, 6-4, and 4-6. (A novice player once asked me, "What about an 8 and a 2?" I said to him, "Sir, if you roll the dice in Las Vegas and they land on an 8 and a 2, you're in big trouble!") There are six ways to roll a 7: 4-3, 3-4, 5-2, 2-5, 6-1, and 1-6.

Think about it. If there are three ways to roll a 10, and six ways to roll a 7, that means the odds are 2-1 that the shooter will roll a 7 before he rolls a 10. By taking the odds, you get paid 2-1 if the shooter makes his 10. Consequently, taking the odds at the dice table is an absolutely even bet (some say the best bet in the casino). The house makes its money on the pass line where winners are paid even money no matter what the point is.

You can take odds on the pass line anytime after the

shooter establishes a point, and you can pick up your odds anytime you wish. You don't even have to tell the dealer.

The odds vary from number to number.

On the 4 and 10, the odds are 2-1. That means for each one unit bet on odds, winners get paid two.

The odds on the 5 and 9 are 3-2. For each two units bet on odds, winners get paid three.

The odds on the 6 and 8 are 6-5. For each five units bet on odds, winners get paid six.

You can also make an odds bet on the don't pass. This is called "laying the odds." Once the shooter establishes a point, the odds are against him making it. So if you're on the don't pass and the shooter has made it past the come-out roll to establish a point, you now have the best of it. Therefore, if you want to bet more money on the don't pass, you have to compensate for this advantage by laying the odds.

Let's look at a point of 10 again. The odds are 2-1 the shooter won't make the 10, which means the odds are 2-1 in your favor if you are on the don't pass. So in order to bet the odds on the don't pass, you have to bet two units to win one. That's one big reason why the don't pass is not as popular as the pass; players don't like to bet more to win less.

Another reason the pass line is more popular is the number of ways you can win on the first roll. There are six ways to roll a 7 and two ways to roll an 11, so out of

**CASINO SECRET**

If you run into trouble at the crap table, just ask one of the dealers for help. For example, ask him, "How much odds can I take?" He'll tell you exactly how much to bet.

36 combinations on the dice you have eight ways of winning your pass line bet on the first roll. On the don't pass, 12 is a standoff. You only win if the first roll is a 2 or 3. There is only one way to roll 2 and two ways to roll 3, so out of 36 combinations you only have three ways of winning your don't pass bet on the first roll.

### Come Bets

The second most popular bet on the dice table is the come bet. Come bets allow you to get money on more numbers, which makes the game a lot more exciting. In fact, the same rules apply to the come bet that apply to the pass line. But unlike a pass line bet that has to be made at the beginning of a sequence on the come-out roll, a come bet can be made at any time. Just put the wager in the come box and the next roll is your come-out. If you make a come bet and the next roll of the dice is a 7 or 11, you win. If the next roll is a craps (2, 3, or 12), you lose. If a point number rolls (4, 5, 6, 8, 9, or 10), your bet "comes" to that number. It stays on that number until either that number rolls again (in which case you win), or until a 7 rolls (in which case you lose).

You can take odds on come bets just like you do on the pass line, and they pay the same way. The one difference is you don't put the odds up yourself. Set the odds down on the come line, where you made your bet originally, and the dealer will place the odds on your bet for you. If you want to take your odds off a come bet during the hand, tell the dealer and he will remove the odds for you. When your bet wins, the dealer takes it off the number and pays it on the come line.

As I mentioned, the reason come bets are so popular is because they afford the opportunity to bet on more numbers during a hand. Rather than just waiting for the shooter to roll his point, you can make come bets and get as many numbers and as much action as you want.

Many experts contend that the best way to play craps

is to bet the pass line and make two come bets…with the odds. The reasoning is, there are only six point numbers, and by making just three bets you can cover half of them. This way is as good as any, and it will keep you from getting caught up in the fever and excitement of the game and getting carried away with your betting. If you want to bet more money, just make larger bets, but three numbers working for you at any one time is enough.

### Don't Come Bets

The don't come is just the opposite of the come. If the first roll is a 7 or 11, your don't come bet loses. If the first roll is a 2 or 3, your don't come bet wins; 12 is a standoff. If the first roll is a point, your money will come behind that point. Now you root for the 7 to roll before the point.

If you want to make an odds bet on your don't come wager, the same rules apply as with the don't pass. Instead of taking the odds, you lay the odds. Consequently, this is not a popular bet.

### Place Bets

You can also bet on the numbers by making place bets. The only problem with place bets is the casino doesn't pay the true amount when you win. The casino pays less than true odds, which is how the house gets its edge. I don't like place bets for that reason.

If you do decide to make place bets, don't try to put the bets up yourself. Instead, place your chips on the come line and tell the dealer which numbers you want to place.

Place the "outside numbers" (the 4, 5, 9, and 10) in units of $5. Place the 6 and 8 in units of $6. Your payoffs are as follows:

- On the 6 and 8, each $6 pays $7.
- On the 5 and 9, each $5 pays $7.
- On the 4 and 10, each $5 pays $9.

You can make a place bet at any time—whether it's a come-out roll or the shooter is in the middle of a hand with a point already established—and you'll have action on the very next roll. If your number rolls before the 7, you win. If the seven rolls first, you lose.

If your place bet hits and you want to double your original bet, tell the dealer to "press it." If you only want to increase your bet by one unit, tell the dealer to "press it one unit."

There are advantages to a place bet. The number only has to roll once and you get paid. You can take a place bet down anytime. And, of course, you get to pick the number you want.

When you make a place bet, you're investing money out of your pocket with the hopes the shooter is going to roll the numbers that you placed before he rolls a loser 7. Let's say, for example, that you decide to place all six numbers. At $5 apiece for the 4, 5, 9 and 10—and $6 apiece for the 6 and 8—you're looking at an investment of $32 ("$32 across"). If the next roll is a loser 7, you lose the whole $32.

Important to remember: when the shooter makes his point and there's a new come-out roll, place bets and odds on come bets are automatically off. You cannot win or lose on the shooter's first roll. If you want to have your bets working on the first roll, tell the dealer and he will place an "on" button on your bets.

On some dice layouts, you will see spaces marked big 6 and big 8. These bets act the same as place bets on the 6 or 8, only you get paid even money, rather than 7-6, when they hit. Never bet on the big 6 or big 8. They are among the worst bets on the table.

## Buy Bets

There is a way of getting paid the true odds on the numbers when you bet them, and that is by making buy bets. The casino, however, charges a 5% commission on the wager. They take the commission in increments of $1, so you must be betting at least $20 to consider this bet.

Buy bets are decided the same way as place bets (you win when your number is rolled before a 7). The commission causes buy bets to have a higher house edge than place bets on the 5, 6, 8, and 9, so you shouldn't consider buying those numbers. On the 4 and 10, however, a buy bet is preferable to a place bet.

### Lay Bets

You can also bet against any number by making a lay bet. As with a buy bet, you must pay a 5% commission. However, the commission on a lay bet is calculated against what you hope to win. Let's say you want to lay $100 against the 4. The odds of a 4 rolling before a 7 are 2-1. Therefore, your $100 wager would only pay $50—less the 5% commission of another $2 (the true commission of $2.50 is usually rounded off in your favor). You are investing $100 to win $48.

If that sounds like a good investment to you, give me a call. I've got some land in Idaho you might be interested in.

### The Field

There is a long oblong box on each end of the table called the field. By betting inside this box, you are betting that the next roll of the dice will be a 2, 3, 4, 9, 10, 11, or 12. If it is, you get paid. It's an even money payoff, except on 2 or 12. If a 2 rolls, you are paid double. If a 12 rolls, you are paid double or triple (depending on the casino). It's a popular bet for novice players because it's so easy, and it looks reasonable with so many winning numbers. Study the field closely, however, and you will notice that most of the good numbers are missing. There is no 5, no 6, no 7, no 8. In fact, of 36 combinations on the dice, 20 of them are not in the field. What's that old expression? If it looks too good to be true, it probably is.

## Proposition Bets

For those who like to smoke cigarettes and drive without wearing seat belts, here's another way to live dangerously. When people ask me, "Are these sucker bets?" I reply, "We don't use the term 'sucker bets' in Las Vegas. We call them *long shots*." But some people don't care; they figure all they have to do is hit a few long shots, and they'll never have to work again. So let's go over all the proposition bets on the table.

The stickman is in charge of these bets. If you want to bet a prop, just toss your money toward the middle of the table and tell the stickman what you want. Make sure he hears you; it's noisy in these casinos. The bets in orange are one-roll bets, including:

**Eleven.** You're betting that the next roll will be 11. If it is, you get paid 16 for 1. That doesn't mean you get $16. You get $15, and your bet is left on the table so you can "win again." If you want all your money, you have to ask for it.

**Any Craps.** You're betting that the next roll will be a 2, 3 or 12. If it is, you get paid 8 for 1.

**C-and-E.** This is craps and 11. Payoffs are the same as above, only you are making one bet that covers both propositions instead of two separate bets. You must bet the table minimum on each wager.

**Horn Bet.** When you make a horn bet, you're betting that the next roll will be a 2, 3, 11, or 12. Since you're betting four different numbers, it costs at least the table minimum for each of the four numbers—$4 if the minimum bet on the props is $1. Some players like to use a $5 chip and bet the extra dollar on one of the four wagers: "Horn high 11," for example. If 3 or 11 rolls, you get paid $16 less your bet (or $32 on the 11 if you bet the extra dollar). If 2 or 12 rolls, you get paid $31 less your bet.

**World Bet.** A world bet is 2, 3, 11, 12, and 7. Payoffs are the same as on a horn bet. If a 7 rolls, you get paid 5 for 1, less your original bet. So if you bet $5 on a world bet and a 7 rolls, you simply break even.

**Any Seven.** As noted above, any seven pays 5 for 1. You can make this wager at any time. One word of caution about betting on 7. Let's say there's a guy about eight feet tall shooting the dice. He's got a point of 4, and you want to bet that he's going to roll a 7. If you holler, "Give me a dollar on 7," he's going to be pretty upset (and downright mad if the 7 rolls). Luckily, there's a secret phrase you can use when you want to bet the 7. It's called "big red." Every dealer in Las Vegas knows what it means. Just say, "Give me a dollar on big red." The shooter won't know what you're betting...and you're betting that he's going to roll that 7!

**The Hardways.** This is one of the most popular proposition bets on the table. There are four numbers on the table that can be rolled "the hard way." They are the 4, 6, 8, and 10. By betting on the hard 8, for example, you are betting the 8 will roll with two 4s. The hardway bets are not displayed in orange, because they are not one-roll wagers. Your bet stays in action until the shooter rolls the hardway, a 7 or an "easy" 8 (which is a 6-2 or a 5-3).

The hard 6 and hard 8 pay 10 for 1. The hard 4 and 10 pay 8 for 1. The reason the hard 6 and 8 pay more is because there are four easy ways to roll those numbers. There are only two ways to roll an easy 4 or 10.

Some players absolutely love the hardways, and they will bet big money on them. I recently taught a young lady how to play craps. When it was her turn to shoot at a real table, she nervously placed a $5 chip on the pass line. Just as she got ready to throw the dice, a man walked up to the other end of the table and bet $1,000 on each of the hardways. The young lady rolled *four* hardways before rolling a loser 7. And every time she rolled a hardway, the man tossed her a $500 chip! She walked away from the table with $2,000. Well, actually she walked away with $1,995. She lost her $5 bet on the pass line.

## Etiquette

Shooting the dice is part of the fun at the crap table. Each person has his own way of doing it. You can shake the dice as hard as you want, blow on them, even set them on a certain number before you let 'em fly. Most casinos, however, ask that you only use one hand when shooting. So rubbing the dice together is a no-no.

Always make your bets while the dice are in the middle of the table. Once the stickman gives the dice to the shooter, no more bets are allowed. Keep your hands out of the playing area once the shooter has the dice. If the dice hit your hand, somebody's liable to hit *you*!

To buy chips at the game, place your money on the table while the dice are in the middle of the layout. (Dealers are not allowed to take money from your hand.) The dealer will set your chips in front of you. Place your chips in the chip rail (the wooden slot that runs around the top of the table). Never leave your chips on the table unless you are betting them.

Before leaving the table, ask the dealer to change all your small chips into larger denominations (known as "coloring up"). Take them to the casino cage for conversion into currency.

You can tip the dealers or make a bet for them, which gives them an opportunity to win extra money. One of the most popular bets for the dealers is on the proposition bets. This is called a "two-way" bet (one way is for you; the other way is for the dealers). To make a two-way bet on the hard 6, for example, just toss two chips to the stickman and say, "Two-way hard 6." Suddenly you'll have made some brand new friends.

## The Casino Advantage

The game's basic bet, the pass-line wager, carries a 1.4% casino advantage. The same applies to the pass-line variations: the don't-pass, come, and don't-come wagers. Using the odds lowers the advantage on the total amount you put into action (line bet plus the odds). The more odds you take, the lower the edge. A line bet with single odds has a casino advantage of .85%. Double odds drops the advantage to .61%. Triple odds is .47%, 10X odds is .18%, and 100X odds (dealt at Binion's Horseshoe, Stratosphere, Sam's Town, and Casino Royale) is a miniscule .02%. Keep in mind, though, in order to take the odds, you must first make a line bet and fade the 1.4% casino edge.

The only other bet on the table that has an edge under 2% is a place bet on the 6 or 8, which carries a casino advantage of 1.5%. Place bets on the 5 or 9 have a casino advantage of 4%. Place bets on the 4 or 10 have an advantage of 6.7%.

Buy bets on 4, 5, 6, 8, 9, or 10 have an edge of 4.8%.

Lay bets carry an edge of 4% on the 6 or 8, 3.2% on the 5 or 9, and 2.4% on the 4 or 10.

The field bet has a 5.6% edge when 12 pays double and 2.8% when 12 pays triple.

A bet on the prominently displayed big 6 or big 8 has an edge of 9.1%.

The hardway bet on 6 or 8 has a 9.1% casino edge. The hardway 4 or 10 is 11.1%

The longshot propositions—2, 3, 11, 12, any craps, c-and-e, horn, world—carry house advantages ranging from 11.1% to 16.67%.

## Crap Talk

Because the stickman has to call every number that's rolled, craps lends itself to flights of language fancy, and over the years lots of slang expressions, rhymes, puns, and strange jargon have entered the dice-table lexicon.

For example, "big red" is slang for 7. For some reason, and don't ask me why, a loser 7 is referred to as "skinny Dugan." When a shooter sevens-out with a 5 and 2, some stickmen like to call "cinco-dos and adios."

"Snake-eyes" and "aces" are slang expressions for 2.

"Yo" means 11. The stickman always calls out 11 as "Yo-leven." Why? In a noisy casino, 7 and 11 sound alike.

Four is "little Joe," 6 is "Jimmy Hicks," two 5s is known as "cherry boxes," 12 is "boxcars" or "midnight," and, of course, there's "eighter from Decatur."

On occasion, players will use jargon to make their bets. Someone who wants to place the 10 and the 4 might say "gimme a Broderick Crawford" (10-4). A place bet on the 5 and the 10 is a "Woolworth."

If some crap shooter tells you that a friend of his "caught ace-deuce," that means his pal died.

The most misused expression in this game is, "He crapped out at the dice table." Not true. A shooter can roll craps and lose his pass line bet, but once a point is established, the only way the shooter loses is by rolling a 7—he "sevens out."

And finally, if you want to talk the talk like a vocabularian, you need to avoid confusing the noun, which is "craps," with the adjective, which is "crap." For example, you say "crap table," "crap dealer," "crap tournament," etc., and not "craps strategy" or "craps system." "Craps" is used as the subject, as in this sentence, or as an object, as in "game of craps"—a noun either way. It's a very common mistake, but now you know the rule.

# 3
# Roulette

## *A Guessing Game*

Roulette dates from the early 19th century, but the game's origins go back to ancient Greece, when soldiers would spin their shields on the points of their swords and bet on where they would stop. In Roman times, it is said that Caesar himself played a form of roulette on a chariot wheel in the palace game room. And then there is Russian roulette, but we won't go into that.

Roulette is French for "little wheel," and what's nice about this game is that you don't have to know a bunch of rules and strategies in order to play. It's strictly a game of chance. There are 38 compartments (or pockets) on the roulette wheel: 36 numbers plus a 0 and 00. The dealer spins a little white ball, and you try to guess in which numbered compartment that little white ball will land.

Roulette attracts a certain type of gambler. It's the one with a whispering hope deep down in his soul that he just might win a lot of money off a very small bet. It's sort of like the lottery, and you have about the same chance of striking it rich in both games. Consequently, only 2% of the people who visit Las Vegas play roulette. But it can be fun, so let's look at all the different bets on the roulette table. Henry, a little mood music, please.

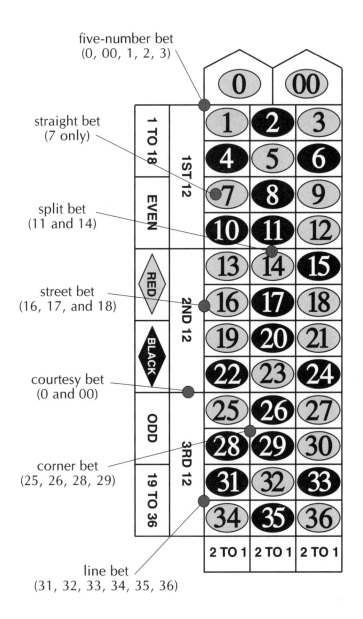

five-number bet
(0, 00, 1, 2, 3)

straight bet
(7 only)

split bet
(11 and 14)

street bet
(16, 17, and 18)

courtesy bet
(0 and 00)

corner bet
(25, 26, 28, 29)

line bet
(31, 32, 33, 34, 35, 36)

## The Outside Bets

Any bet outside the 38 individual numbers is called an "outside" bet. The most popular of these are the six bets on the edge of the layout closest to you. By placing your bet in the square marked "1 to 18," you are betting that the next slot the ball drops into on the wheel will be any number from 1 to 18. By placing your money in the square marked "19 to 36," you are betting any number on the other half of the layout. Both bets pay even money.

If you bet in the "odd" square, you are betting that any odd number will come up on the next spin of the wheel. You can bet that an even number will show by betting in the "even" square. These bets also pay even money.

You can also bet in the squares marked "red" and "black." Eighteen of the numbers are red, and 18 are black, so each of these pays even money.

By betting in the square marked "1st 12," you are covering the first 12 numbers. Winners are paid 2-1. Payoffs are the same for the squares marked "2nd 12" and "3rd 12."

You may also make what is called a "column" bet. Now you are betting any number in a column of 12 numbers, and again the payoff is 2-1.

On any outside bet, your winnings are placed next to the original wager.

## The Inside Bets

Any bet on the individual numbers is called an "inside" bet. There are several different ways you can bet on these numbers.

You can bet on one number, which is called a "straight" bet. If that number comes up on the next spin, you get paid 35-1. By the way, the most popular number on the wheel is 17. Why? It's right in the center of the table for one thing, and it's the number that James Bond always bets in the movies. Well, he never loses, does he?

You can also cover two numbers with one chip. This is called a "split" bet, and it pays 17-1 if either number shows. If you can't reach the numbers you want to bet on, set the chip on the table in front of you and tell the dealer where you want it. He will place it for you.

Many players like to bet a chip on the 0-00 split. That way, if either 0 or 00 comes up, they will lose their other bets on the table—but they'll get paid 17-1 for the 0-00 split. It's like a little insurance policy, a way of protecting other bets on the table in case 0 or 00 does appear.

For those who can't reach the 0-00, there is a courtesy bet on the table. It's located on the white line between "2nd 12" and "3rd 12." By placing a bet on that white line, it's the same thing as betting on 0-00. This is the only courtesy bet on the layout.

Another popular inside bet is covering three numbers with one chip. Also known as a "street" bet, it pays 11-1. The numbers must run vertically. Place your bet on the white line between the outside bets and the row of three numbers that you want.

A "corner" bet is a bet on four numbers. The numbers must be in a group of four, and you place the chip so it touches the corners of all four numbers. The payoff on this popular bet is 8-1.

There is one place on the table where you can cover five numbers with one chip. By placing your bet on the white line between "1st 12" and the 1 and 0, you are betting the next number that comes up on the wheel will be 0, 00, 1, 2 or 3. If any of these five numbers come up, you get paid 6-1. (Stay away from this one. The house edge on this particular wager is the highest of any on the table: 7.89%.)

Finally, you can cover six numbers with one chip. This is called a "line" bet. Place your chip on the white line between the outside bets and the two rows of numbers you want. This bet pays 5-1.

A simple way to calculate your payoff on any inside

bet is to divide the number of numbers you are covering into 36, and then subtract one. For example, if you bet on four numbers, divide 4 into 36. Then from your answer of 9, subtract 1. Your total is 8, and thus your payoff is 8 to 1. This works with all inside bets except the five-number bet.

On any inside bet, winnings are paid in front of you, and your original bet stays where it is. If you don't want to make the bet again, it's up to you to pick up your money.

## Basic Strategy

There is none. Roulette is nothing more than an old carnival game. You're hoping a little ball is going to stop where you want it to. Don't listen when some roulette player tells you about a sure-fire way to beat the game. Forget about systems and strategies and how-to books. Most of them are a complete waste of time and money.

One myth that refuses to die is about veteran dealers who have spun the ball so many times in their illustrious careers that they develop a pattern of motion and speed. The assumption is that the ball will land in a certain section more often than not. And what if the roulette wheel is slightly tilted? What if the divider separating one number from another on the wheel is worn slightly more than the other dividers? What if the ball jumps off the wheel and hits you right in the eyeball? The odds of that happening are about the same as any of these other scenarios.

Casinos go to great lengths to ensure that the roulette wheel is mechanically sound in every way. There is even a compass on most tables to make sure that nobody slips a metal ball into the game.

Some players "clock" roulette wheels, looking for repeat numbers—then bet numbers that seem to come in more often than they ought to. This is known as playing a "bias." There's nothing wrong with it, because if it doesn't work, you haven't increased the house edge any more than it was originally. In fact, most casinos supply score cards so you can track each number that comes up on the wheel. Some casinos even have electronic reader boards that show the last 21 winning numbers.

What is the house edge at roulette? On a wheel with both a 0 and a 00, the casino has a built-in edge of 5.26%. If you are going to play roulette, look for a wheel with only a single 0. The house edge drops to only 2.7%. All roulette wheels in European casinos use the single-zero wheel (many also have a rule called "en prison," which cuts the edge on even-money wagers to 1.35%), and that is why the game is so popular there. In Las Vegas, the Monte Carlo casino has single-zero roulette wheels. So does Stratosphere. The Reserve has two roulette wheels, both single-zero.

Still another option available on some roulette tables is called a "neighbors" bet. Many players like to track the wheel, their idea being that if a certain number comes up on one roll, the ball just might land in the same cluster of numbers on the next. With a neighbors bet, you bet on one number and the two numbers on either side of that number. For example, these five numbers are next to one another on the wheel: 36, 24, 3, 15, and 34. To make a neighbors bet on these numbers, place your money on the table and tell the dealer, "Give me 3 and the neighbors." If any of the five numbers in that cluster come up on the next spin, you get paid 35 to 1. Since you're betting five numbers, however, you have to wager five times as much.

Most people who play roulette usually bet on the same numbers all the time. Some people bet on their birthday; others bet on the date of their anniversary. In fact, here is a story that is supposed to have happened in one Vegas casino. A young woman was playing roulette with her boyfriend.

"What number should I bet on?" she asked him.

"Oh, just bet on your age."

She placed a chip on number 23. The ball landed on 29—and she fainted!

## Etiquette

Roulette is the only game in the casino where each player has his own color of chips. That's so you can keep track of your bets. You can have any color that is not being used by another player.

Roulette chips are only negotiable at the roulette wheel. This is because there is no dollar value indicated on the chips; the value of your chips is determined by the amount you pay for them. So exchange your "wheel chips" for regular casino chips before leaving the table.

Each player is responsible for the correct positioning of his wagers on the layout. Even if the dealer or another player helps you place bets that you cannot reach, it is still up to you to make certain your bets are placed correctly.

When making your bets, be careful not to reach over the casino's chips (or rack, as it is called). There are people out there who make a living by stealing chips, so for security reasons you will be watched closely if your hands stray too close to the chip rack. At one Vegas casino, a man played for five hours, and finally the dealer quit paying attention to him. When the player left the table, six $5,000 chips were missing. He'd grabbed them when nobody was watching. The man was never caught, but the dealer lost his job.

You can place your bets at any time, even after the dealer has spun the ball. Eventually, though, the ball will start to slow down. At this point, the dealer will announce, "No more bets." That's when you stop playing and start praying.

# 4
# Baccarat

## *Easier to Play Than It Is To Say*

Baccarat (BAH-ka-rah) is an old game usually played by old people with old-world money. It's about as exciting as watching paint dry, but—darn it—it's one of the best games you can play. Invented by the Romans, refined by the French, and generally ignored by the Americans, it is purely a guessing game like roulette. The odds against you, however, are much lower.

Baccarat is usually played in a private area of the casino. Dealers wear tuxedos and security guards are posted just outside the velvet ropes, the muted light from the chandeliers softly shimmering off the barrels of their automatic submachine guns.

Like other casino table games it is intimidating, and consequently less than 1% of the people who frequent casinos play baccarat. That's a shame, because once you get over that initial fear, you'll find that baccarat is a neat little game.

Eight decks of cards are used, but don't let that worry you. You couldn't count cards in this game if you tried, and it wouldn't matter anyway. You're just trying to guess which hand will be closest to 9: the banker or the player. The dealer is not the banker, and strange as it sounds, you are not the player. These are just the names of the hands. You can bet on either hand by placing your

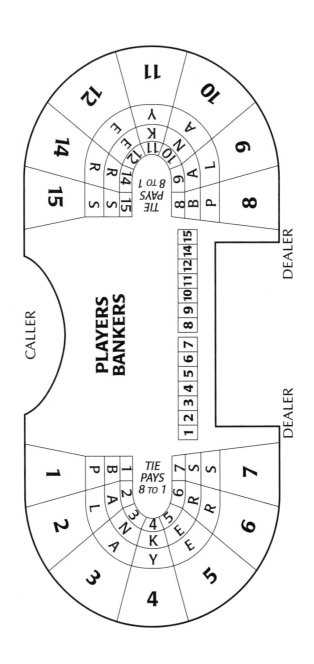

wager in one of the appropriate boxes in front of you.

The cards have the following values: aces count as 1, face cards and 10s count as zero, the other cards (2 through 9) are counted at face value. All the cards are added together and only the last digit is counted. Example: A 9 and 4 are dealt to the player. They add up to 13, but only the last digit is counted—3. So as you can see, the total will never be more than 9. Once the total reaches 10, it goes back to zero again.

Each player gets a chance to deal the cards. It's just part of the razzmatazz and gives the game its Monte Carlo flavor. You simply slide a card face down out of the shoe for the player, then a card for the banker. Now one more card for the player, and one more for the banker.

The cards for the banker are tucked under the shoe, and the player with the shoe passes the player's hand to the dealer. The dealer will give the player's hand to the person at the table making the largest bet on the player, and he will turn the cards over. If no one is betting on the player, then the dealer will expose the cards. When directed by the dealers, the person with the shoe exposes the banker's cards.

• If the player's first two cards total less than 6, the player will take one additional card.
• If the player's first two cards total 6 or more, the player will not take another card.
• If either the player's first two cards or the banker's two cards total 8 or 9, it's called a "natural" and no more cards are dealt.
• If the hand ends in a tie, it's a push and no money changes hands. As soon as the player wins a hand, the shoe goes to the next participant in the game.

In the event the player takes another card, the dealer will say, "One more card for the player." So the person with the shoe really has no decisions to make. All he is doing is dealing the cards, and that's what makes the game so easy.

The banker may take an additional card, or may not. It all depends upon what the player's cards are. In the long run you have a better chance of winning by betting on the banker. Therefore, when you bet on the banker and win, you must pay a 5% commission. That's how the house makes its money at baccarat.

Taking the commission into account, the banker is still a better bet. The house edge is only 1.06%. The house edge when you bet on the player is 1.24%. In other words, the banker bet is just a little worse than flipping a coin.

As far as the commission is concerned, the dealer will keep track of it, and everybody settles up when all the cards are dealt from the shoe. So keep an extra $100 in *your* shoe, so you have enough to pay.

In one plush Las Vegas casino, a wealthy Asian strolled into the baccarat pit. This particular player was so rich he was allowed to bet $250,000 a hand. (The maximum bet for us peons is usually $5,000.) The casino, of course, was figuring the man would win half his bets and lose half his bets, so it would pick up quite a piece of change in commissions. After all, 5% of 250 grand is $12,500. Unfortunately for the casino, the man could do no wrong, and when he left eight hours later, he took $18 million of the casino's money with him. It was one of the biggest wins in casino history, and caused the company's stock to plummet on Wall Street. However, the same player came back a few weeks later…and guess what happened?

### The Third Card Rule

The only complicated aspect of baccarat is known as "the third card rule." This applies only to the banker's hand.

Again, the rules for the player's hand are quite simple. The player, having less than 6, takes another card. With

6 or 7, the player stands. An 8 or 9 is a natural, and the banker cannot draw. That's it.

But for the banker the following set of complicated rules apply:

• If the banker's first two cards total 0, 1, or 2, the banker will take an additional card.
• If the banker's first two cards total 3, the banker takes an additional card unless the player draws an 8.
• If the banker's first two cards total 4, the banker takes an additional card unless the player's third card is an ace, 8, 9, or 10.
• If the banker's first two cards total 5, the banker takes an additional card unless the player's third card is an ace, 2, 3, 8, 9, or 10.
• If the banker's first two cards total 6, the banker takes an additional card unless the player's third card is an ace, 2, 3, 4, 5, 8, 9, or 10.
• If the banker's first two cards total 7, the banker stands.
• If the banker's first two cards total 8 or 9, it is a natural and the player cannot draw.
• If the player takes no cards, the banker stands on 6.

There is an easy way to memorize the third card rule. The way I did it was like this. If the banker has a total of 4, banker draws when the player's next card is 2 through 7. With a total of 5, banker draws if player's third card is 4 through 7. If banker has 6, banker draws if player's third card is 6 or 7.

If you don't want to bother learning this part of the game, let the dealer worry about it. He knows what to do.

Note: On each baccarat table, you will see a box containing score cards and pens. These are furnished so that you may track each hand that is played. It doesn't really mean anything, but just about everybody does it. "Hey, the player just won five hands in a row. Looks like it's time for the banker to win a hand. FIVE THOUSAND ON THE BANKER!" Now you know why everyone is busy scribbling away at the table.

## Ties

There is one proposition bet on the table where you may bet that the hand ends in a tie. If a tie occurs, you're paid 8-1. Statistically, a tie comes up in baccarat once every 10.5 hands, which means the casino has a 14.4% edge. It isn't a very popular bet.

## Etiquette

People who play baccarat generally have more money than the rest of us, so etiquette at this game is a bit more refined.

Do not eat beluga caviar at the table. Eating food at a gaming table is frowned upon by management. Instead, have your personal chauffeur pull the stretch limo around to the side entrance of the casino. Your personal maid can then deliver the caviar to your personal valet, who will prepare your dining table in the casino owner's office. His desk will do just fine.

On the other hand, it is perfectly permissible to sip Dom Perignon champagne while you play. When finished, however, please refrain from smashing your glass in the fireplace. First of all, broken glass can be dangerous to the other patrons. Secondly, there are no fireplaces in casinos.

If you lose a few million at the table, please do not buzz the casino in your Lear jet.

# Mini-Baccarat

Mini-baccarat is a pocket-sized version of the big game. It's becoming more and more popular because you can play for lower stakes. The same rules apply in mini-baccarat as in baccarat, with the following exceptions:

• In mini-baccarat, the dealer deals all the cards.
• Commissions are settled more often.
• The table is much smaller and is located with other games in the pit.
• The table minimums are lower.
• The game is played at a much faster pace.

# 5
# Pai Gow Poker

## *Push, Push, Win, Push, Push, Lose, Push, Lose*

This is a relatively new game, and it's rapidly becoming a casino favorite. It's based on the ancient Chinese game of pai gow, but is played with a deck of playing cards instead of tiles. Actually, the game is a combination of pai gow and good old American poker, so if you can play poker, you can play pai gow poker. If you can't play poker, you can still play pai gow poker—after you read my list of all the winning poker hands—starting with the best hand you can make.

• five aces (there is one joker in the deck that can be used as an ace)
• royal flush (ace, king, queen, jack, 10 in the same suit; the joker can also be used as a wild card to complete any straight or flush)
• straight flush (any five-card run: 2, 3, 4, 5, 6, for example, of the same suit)
• four-of-a-kind (four kings, four 3s, etc.)
• full house (three-of-a-kind and a pair)
• flush (five cards of the same suit)
• straight (any five-card run)
• three-of-a-kind
• two pair
• one pair
• high card

Now that you know the winning poker hands, let's play pai gow poker. The dealer deals the cards into seven hands with seven cards in each hand. (The remaining four cards are placed in the discard rack for the remainder of the hand.)

The dealer then shakes the dice bowl, which contains three dice. This is to determine who receives the first hand. The numbers on the three dice are totaled, and the dealer counts counterclockwise around the table, starting from the dealer's position, determining who gets which hand based on the dice total. This is to ensure random distribution of the cards, and it's part of the Oriental flavor of the game.

Each player then arranges the seven cards dealt to him into two separate hands: five cards in his highest hand and two cards in his second highest hand. Once the two hands are formed, each player places his cards face down in the positions indicated on the layout.

After each player has set his two hands, the dealer turns his cards over and sets his two hands the same way: five cards in his highest hand, two in his second highest hand. Now the dealer turns the other hands over one at a time, starting with the player on the dealer's immediate right.

In order to win, both your hands must beat both the dealer's hands. In order to lose, both your hands must lose to both the dealer's hands. If you win one hand and lose one hand, it is a push, and no money changes hands.

Keep in mind that your second highest (two-card) hand has to be lower than your highest (five-card) hand, and that is the only hard rule you must follow. If you make your second highest hand higher than your highest hand, it is called a "foul hand," and you lose automatically.

Here is the secret of how to win at pai gow poker in one short sentence. Make your second highest hand as high as you can—as long as your highest hand is higher!

Sample hand. The dealer deals you two 6s, two jacks, a 7, 9, and 10. Playing regular poker, it would make sense to keep your two pair together. If you did that in pai gow poker, however, your other hand would probably lose, and you would wind up with a push. In pai gow poker, the proper way to play this hand is to place the two jacks in your highest hand (along with your 7, 9, and 10), and the two 6s in your second highest hand. Now you have a good chance of winning both hands.

Sample hand. The dealer deals you three 5s, two 7s, an ace, and a 4. Place your three 5s in your highest hand (with the ace and 4), and the two 7s in your second highest hand. You are making your second highest hand as high as you can, but your highest hand is still higher.

Or let's say the dealer really likes you and deals you two aces, two 10s, two 8s and a jack. In this case, you should place the two 10s, the two 8s and the jack in your highest hand, and the two aces in your second highest hand. Two pair is a good hand, and nothing will beat two aces in a two-card hand.

Rule of thumb: If you have two pair, always split by placing your high pair in your highest hand and your low pair in your second highest hand.

Exception: If one pair is lower than 7s, and you have an odd ace, play the low pair with the high pair and play your ace in the second highest hand. You have a strong combination in your highest hand, and an ace with any other card is still a good two-card hand.

Points to remember: Be careful not to foul or you could forfeit your bet. If you're not sure how to set your hand, ask the dealer to set it for you. He is not doing you a favor. It's part of the game.

The joker can only be used as an ace, or as a wild card in a straight or flush. When used in a straight or flush, it will fill in as the highest card possible.

I really like this game and I'll tell you why. First of all, it's slow-moving. By the time the dealer shuffles the cards, deals, shakes the dice bowl, distributes the cards to the players, waits for each player to set his hand, sets his hand, then turns over each hand and pays each winning bet—my gosh, three or four minutes have gone by. Meanwhile, you're gambling; you're racking up all sorts of casino amenities; and you're hardly losing any money!

Look back at the sub-head at the beginning of this chapter. Understand it now? Pai gow poker incorporates a lot of pushes. In truth, the pushes aren't quite as common as the sub-head suggests. Statistics indicate that the game will end in a tie 45% of the time. What this means is you usually won't win a lot of money playing pai gow poker, but you usually won't lose a lot of money, either.

You are probably wondering how the casino makes any money at this game. After all, you get seven cards, and the dealer gets seven cards. You have just as good a chance of winning as the dealer, right? Not quite, because the dealer wins copies. When one of your two hands ties the dealer's, it's called a copy. They usually occur in the two-card hand (i.e., ace-jack for you and ace-jack for the dealer). But the main way the casino makes its money is via a commission on winners—when you win both hands, you must pay the house a 5% commission. Then again, the casino is furnishing the plush surroundings, the drinks, the music, the good-looking dealers. Let them have their commission; you're having fun.

Don't worry about how to pay the commission. The dealer will take it out of your payoff. There is no commission on losing bets or pushes.

One day I was teaching a group of people the finer points of pai gow poker. One of those taking part was a well-dressed woman of about 60. From her appearance and overall demeanor, it was obvious that she came from a distinguished lineage, probably heralding from some fancy place like Boston or Philadelphia. She was seated at the table, listening with a haughty tilt of her head as I explained the intricacies of the game. Then I got to the commission.

"So when you win both hands," I said, "you must pay the casino a 5% commission."

"Five percent?" she exploded. "Why, that sucks!"

## House Ways

The only rule you must follow is that your highest hand be higher than your second highest hand. However, the dealer must play his cards according to "house way(s)." You do not have to play this way, but if the dealer has to play a certain way, there must be a reason for it—in pai gow poker, it's usually the right way to play.

• No pair: Use the second and third highest ranked cards for the second highest hand.
• One pair: Always play the pair in the highest hand, and use the next two highest cards in the second highest hand.
• Two pair: Always split, and place the high pair in the highest hand and the low pair in the second highest hand. The only exception is if one pair is lower than 7s, and you have an odd ace. Then keep the two pair together and play the ace in your second highest hand.
• Three pair: Always play the highest pair in the second highest hand.
• Three-of-a-kind: Always keep in the highest hand, unless aces. Then play one of the aces in the second highest hand.
• Full house: Always split and play pair in second highest hand.
• Three-of-a-kind and two pair: Play highest pair in second highest hand.
• Four-of-a-kind: Never split 2s through 6s. Play in highest hand. Split 7s through 10s, unless ace can be played in second highest hand. Always split face cards and aces.

Again, if you don't want to bother learning the house ways, just ask the dealer to set your hand for you. He can do it in his sleep (and sometimes does).

## Being the Banker

Another exciting aspect of pai gow poker is that any player can be the banker. The dealer is usually the banker, and this is indicated by a small plastic marker called a "chung," which the dealer places on top of his cards after dealing. If you wish to be the banker, just tell the dealer before the cards are dealt and he will place the chung in your betting circle.

The advantage to being the banker is that you win the copies. The disadvantage to being the banker is that you have to book the action of all the other players at the table. If you get a losing hand, you have to pay everyone else, including the dealer.

Points to remember: In order to be the banker, you must have enough money on the table to pay all winning bets.

**CASINO SECRET**

If you are the only player at a pai gow poker table, be the banker as often as you can. Since the banker wins all tie hands, it is to your advantage to bank. The dealer's wager will be the amount of your last bet, so you won't be at risk for any more money than you would be as a regular player. Or at your request, the dealer will bet the table minimum. As far as the 5% commission is concerned, the house still gets it—whether you're the banker or not. (You might not want to bank if there are other players—you'll be responsible for covering their bets, too.)

You may be the banker for one hand only. Then the bank reverts back to the dealer for the next hand.

## Etiquette

At pai gow poker, it is considered proper etiquette to wait for the dealer to put down the dice bowl before looking at your cards. And when you're the banker, you should wait for the other players to set their hands before you set yours.

Avoid exposing your cards at the table. It doesn't matter when the dealer is the banker, because the dealer must follow house ways. When another player is the banker, however, you will be giving him an advantage if he sees how you set your hand.

# Pai Gow

If you see a game in the casino being played by Asians, dealt by Asians, and supervised by Asians, it will probably be pai gow. This is the game on which pai gow poker is based and it has practically been a national institution in China since the 12th century.

Literally translated, pai gow means "to make nine," which has something to do with the object of the game. Thirty-two domino-shaped tiles are used. The dealer shuffles them and places them into eight stacks, four tiles in each, which he distributes to the players. Or is it four stacks with eight in each?

Anyway, the values of the tiles are not based on the number of dots, but on symbolic Chinese rankings, such as "bo," "wong," "gong," and "gee joon." Consequently, no one from outside China knows how to play pai gow. If someone wins, the casino has to take his word for it.

"Are you sure you won?"

"Yes!"

"Okay. Here's your money."

Now that you thoroughly understand the game, I will tell you how you can walk away from a pai gow table with $1,000. (You start with $2,000...)

Suggestion: Stick with pai gow poker. It's much easier to learn and simpler to play.

# 6
# Slot Machines

## *One Spin Can Change Your Life*

Gambling is America's favorite pastime. More Americans gamble than go to movies, theater, opera, and concerts combined. Americans spend six times as much money on gambling as on all spectator sports put together, or enough to run the U.S. State Department for four years. And when most people gamble, they choose one form of gambling above all others—the shiny, chrome-plated, bell-ringing, light-flashing, coin-guzzling slot machine.

Slot machines are quick, they're simple, they're non-threatening, and they pack a potentially big payback. Psychiatrists say they also offer instant gratification and an intense rapid-fire experience. As a result, each casino generates close to two-thirds of its revenue from these mechanical marvels.

Years ago, slot machines were called one-armed bandits, and your chances of winning anything were practically nil. Today some slots—such as Megabucks, Cool Millions, Quartermania, Dollars Deluxe, Fabulous Fifties, and High Rollers—can turn you into an instant millionaire with just one pull of the handle.

In fact, if I were going to play a slot machine, these hybrids with the potentially life-altering jackpots are the kind I would play. Chances are you're going to lose anyway, so why not take a flyer at the big payoff? Unfortunately, these progressive machines take away many of the smaller jackpots in exchange for the chance to hit the big one. So it's a matter of personal choice. Do you want to play for hours and maybe hit a jackpot for a couple of thousand dollars? Or do you want to buck the big odds and go for a fortune...and probably go broke? It's up to you.

I've noticed over the years that the people who win the really big jackpots on machines such as Megabucks have only invested $15 or $20 before striking it rich. While this has no bearing on your chances, it serves to illustrate an important point: don't play with the idea that if you put enough money into a machine you're going to hit the thing, or that if someone leaves a machine without winning you have a better chance yourself. It all comes down to being lucky—playing the right machine at the right moment in time.

Take the college student who won $10.9 million on a Megabucks slot machine in 1996. He'll pick up $438,000 a year for the next 25 years. Stories like this whet every gambler's appetite, and that's just what the developers of Megabucks want. The developers happen to be IGT (International Game Technology), and they have a network of more than 700 Megabucks machines in almost 150 Nevada casinos. Originally, the Megabucks jackpot started at $1 million, and went up fractionally every time someone played one. Several years later the machines

> **CASINO SECRET**
>
> Theft is the number one crime in Las Vegas casinos. When playing a slot machine, watch your purse and other valuables. If you must set your purse down, make sure there is a wall or partition between your machine and others in the same carousel. Otherwise, keep your purse in your lap.

were reset at $3 million after a jackpot was hit, and now the machines are reset at $5 million.

IGT won't tell anyone how many stops there are on each of the three reels of a Megabucks slot machine, but slot manufacturers today use a microprocessor chip that provides hundreds of stops per reel. For the sake of argument, let's say that IGT only programs 100 stops on each Megabucks reel. Multiply 100 X 100 X 100, and that should give you some idea what your chances are of hitting this baby. For the long haul, you're better off sticking to slot machines that don't offer you the moon.

Non-progressive slot machines (with fixed awards based on the number of coins played) can give you more play for your money, because they have more frequent payouts than progressive machines. The fact is, most Nevada casinos pay back around 97% on straight dollar reel machines, around 92% on quarter reel machines, and around 85% on nickel reel machines. What this means is if you play the larger denomination machines, the casino gives you more of your money back.

**Always play the maximum number of coins.** Often, slot machines deliver a bonus on jackpots hit with the maximum number of coins played. For example, Megabucks players only qualify for the giant progressive if they make the maximum bet ($3). Imagine the lifetime of heartache if you happened to line up four Megabucks symbols on the pay line with only one or two coins in. Instead of winning millions of dollars, you'd win a lowly secondary jackpot, at best (some machines wouldn't even pay that).

**In Las Vegas, play downtown.** Generally, downtown slots have a higher payback than slots anywhere else. Cheap meals and loose slots are Fremont Street's way of competing with the fancier hotels on the Strip.

Always carry identification in the casino. Without proper ID, you won't get paid for a jackpot over $1,200. The IRS requires taxes to be paid on slot machine winnings over $1,200 and on keno winnings over $1,500. If you don't have ID, the casino will withhold payment.

**Join a slot club.** Most casinos have slot clubs. You are issued a card that you use each time you play the slots, and you can often use the card on the table games, too. By using a slot club card, you're allowing the casino to track exactly how much money you play through a slot machine; when you've played a certain number of coins (usually $10-$20), you get a point. You'll be surprised how quickly your points add up, and you'll be eligible for all kinds of casino bonuses: gifts, cash, meals, shows, and discounted room rates. (When playing the machines, make sure your slot card is inserted properly—and don't forget to take it with you when you leave!)

Even if you don't plan to play the machines, joining a slot club is still worth the effort. Some casinos give you a free gift just for joining. A good book to read is Jeffrey Compton's *The Las Vegas Advisor Guide to Slot Clubs.*

If you don't want to stand in line, try to sign up at a slot club booth before 10 a.m. Mornings are notoriously slow in casinos.

Make sure to play on holidays or special occasions, such as Mother's Day or Valentine's Day. Most slot clubs offer double points on these occasions.

No matter if you have a winning or losing session, you're always racking up points on your club card, and your Hawaiian vacation prize is that much closer to becoming a reality. The only problem is what you'll do for spending money when you get there—you put all your money in the machines!

---

**CASINO SECRET**

Before leaving a slot machine, make sure all credits have been used and check your coin tray for stray coins. Check other machines around you, too. Some people make a living doing this.

# 7
# Video Poker

## *Study Pays*

Video poker is truly the game of the decade. This game, which combines the skill of draw poker with the ease of playing a machine, has literally exploded in popularity. The player is not just "pouring money down the hungry gullet of a plain slot machine," as Dwight Crevelt writes in his book *Video Poker Mania*. He is making choices that "give the player a sensation of control and power over the outcome. The player is not entirely at the machine's mercy."

Video poker was first introduced in 1976, when a few machines were installed on an experimental basis at Sam's Town. The industry was astonished by the results. Players waited in line for a spot at one of the twelve machines, itching to test their skill against modern technology. It's a love affair that has never waned. Ask my wife. She loves the 25¢ deuces wild machines, because she doesn't have to hit a royal flush in order to win something. All she needs are four deuces and she goes home with $250—plus all those wonderful points from the slot club.

Frankly, you're better off butting heads with a video poker machine than playing in one of the city's smoky poker rooms. For one thing, the house takes a rake from each poker pot. For another, professional poker players make a good living preying on unsuspecting amateurs. In an interview, professional baseball player Greg Maddux, one of the many celebrities who live in Vegas, addressed the caliber of the locals in the poker rooms. "They play poker 10 hours a day. The more you do anything, the better you get at it, and these guys are good, man." Sounds like Greg's been on the wrong end of a few no-hitters himself.

You don't have to know how to play poker in order to play video poker; the winning hands and payouts are printed right on the award glass. Example:

## Deuces Wild Schedule

*Payoffs correspond to the first column on the award glass.*

| | |
|---|---|
| Royal flush | 250 (4,000 max coins) |
| Four deuces | 200 coins |
| Royal flush with deuces | 25 coins |
| Five-of-a-kind | 15 coins |
| Straight flush | 9 coins |
| Four-of-a-kind | 5 coins |
| Full house | 3 coins |
| Flush | 2 coins |
| Straight | 2 coins |
| Three-of-a-kind | 1 coin |

## Deuces Wild Strategy

If you play deuces wild with optimum strategy against the pay schedule that appears above, you can expect a return of 100.7% (long-term). In deuces wild, the most important card is the deuce; always keep every deuce you're dealt. What you hold besides the deuces depends on how many deuces you start out with. The following is an abbreviated strategy that will help guide you.

**If you're dealt 3 deuces:**
• Throw away anything that doesn't give you a made royal flush or five-of-a-kind. The worst you can do with this strategy is wind up with four-of-a-kind.

**If you're dealt 2 deuces:**
• Keep a made four-of-a-kind or better, four cards to a royal flush (i.e., two deuces plus 10, jack suited), and four consecutive cards to a straight flush if 6 or higher (i.e., two deuces plus 6, 7 suited).
• Throw away made straights and flushes (not straight flushes) and draw to the two deuces only.

**If you're dealt 1 deuce:**
• Keep all combinations that pay (three-of-a-kind or higher).
• Keep three cards to a royal (i.e., the deuce plus jack, king suited).
• Keep three consecutive cards to a straight flush if they are 6 or higher (i.e., the deuce plus 6, 7 suited).

**If you're dealt 0 deuces:**
• Keep all combinations that pay (three-of-a-kind or higher).
• Keep four cards to a flush or straight (including inside straights).
• Keep three cards to a straight flush or royal flush (even if not consecutive).
• Keep a single pair (if dealt two pair, keep only one of them).

Otherwise draw five new cards. Also, remember to always play maximum coins.

There are several additional strategy refinements for playing deuces wild. If you want to edge closer to getting that 100.7% return, pick up the books *Winning Strategies for Video Poker* by Lenny Frome or *Video Poker—Pre-*

*cision Play* by Dan Paymar. Another good way to perfect your play is with a computer program; the best one is *Video Poker Tutor.*

There are also many other deuces wild pay-schedule variations. The important variations take place in the payoffs for a wild royal flush, five-of-a-kind, straight flush, and four-of-a-kind. The books mentioned above will help you differentiate between the good and bad machines.

### Jacks or Better

Below is a schedule for your basic jacks or better non-progressive video poker machine. The main reason for its popularity is that a pair of jacks returns your original bet. Mathematically speaking, this happens about 20% of the time. I don't think it's as exciting as deuces wild, because the only chance you have of winning anything big is to hit a royal—and how often is that going to happen? Once every 40,000 hands or so.

### Jacks or Better Schedule

*(Payoffs correspond to the first column on the award glass.)*

| | |
|---|---|
| Royal flush | 250 (4,000 max coins) |
| Straight flush | 50 coins |
| Four-of-a-kind | 25 coins |
| Full house | 9 coins |
| Flush | 6 coins |
| Straight | 4 coins |
| Three-of-a-kind | 3 coins |
| Two pair | 2 coins |
| One pair/jacks or better | 1 coin |

### Jacks or Better Strategy

If you play jacks or better with optimum strategy against the pay schedule that appears above, you can expect a return of greater than 99% (long term). The secret of winning at jacks or better is to stay in action until you hit the royal, so follow these simple guidelines.

### Draw 1 Card

If you have four cards to a royal flush, four cards to a straight flush, four cards to a flush or straight (and no high pair), or two pair.

### Draw 2 Cards

If you have three-of-a-kind, or if you have no high pair but have three cards to a royal flush or three consecutive cards to a straight flush (draw three to a low pair over the straight flush draw).

### Draw 3 Cards

If you have any pair, or two high cards. With three high cards to choose from, first keep any two that are suited, then the two lowest. Keep three high cards only if they are jack, queen, king of different suits. (Choose a pair over any two high cards.)

### Draw 4 Cards

If you have one high card.

### Draw 5 Cards

If you don't have at least a high card or three consecutive cards to a straight flush.

Don't keep kickers (a high card along with a pair); don't draw to inside straights; and always play maximum coins.

This, too, is a cursory strategy. The books by Frome and Paymar mentioned earlier will help you to play more accurately.

Just as important as playing your cards right is finding a good pay schedule. The first thing you should do before you sit down at a jacks or better machine is look at the payoffs for the full house and flush on the award glass. The payout for a full house should be 9 coins per coin played; the payout for a flush should be 6 coins per coin played. This is known as a "9/6 machine." Do not play jacks or better machines that pay 8 (or 7 or 6) coins for a full house and 5 for a flush. Their overall return is about $2^{1}/_{4}$ % less.

Even sticking to the good machines, though, you won't win every time you play. That's why there are 2,768,912 pawn shops in Las Vegas. As Dwight Crevelt writes in his book *Video Poker Mania*: "For every person who achieves royal status, there are hundreds of thousands who are never touched by that magic wand."

# 8
# Other Games

## Caribbean Stud, Let It Ride, Casino War, Big Six, Race & Sports Book, Bingo, Keno

The casinos of today are nothing like those of the Bugsy Siegel era. Corporations have tried to peel away the cloak of vice and intrigue associated with earlier casinos, but I think there was a certain aura of glamour about those times. It felt almost like you were breaking the law when you gambled. And even though you weren't breaking the law, at least there was the slight chance that you might actually bump into a real gangster. It made your trip a unique experience that incorporated a sort of reckless bravado that you would always remember.

Today, a visit to a casino is like a trip to an amusement park. In fact, most casinos *are* amusement parks and gambling is an E-ticket attraction. Yet there's still a shady tinge to it all, which doesn't sit too well with some of the big corporations. Consequently, most casinos today require their supervisors to wear dark suits and conservative ties. They try to make it seem more like you're in a bank than in a gambling joint.

Of course, in order to get to the white tiger display or the snazzy shopping arcade, you still have to walk past all those dice tables and slot machines. If you don't like those, how about Caribbean Stud or Let It Ride? The casinos have introduced a whole batch of new games, figuring there's bound to be one that you'll like. Some of them are even fun.

So gentlemen—start your ATM machines!

# Caribbean Stud

This game was first tried on an experimental basis aboard cruise ships and was so successful that it can now be found in most Nevada casinos. Each player antes, then is dealt five cards from a regular 52-card deck. The dealer also gets five cards and turns one over. After seeing this card, you must decide whether you want to stay in the game, or fold. If you fold, you lose your ante. If you decide to stay, you must double your ante by making a separate wager called a "call bet."

The dealer then reveals his remaining four cards. If the dealer does not "qualify" by having at least an ace and king, the hand is over and each player who called wins the amount of his ante. If the dealer does qualify, the hand is played to completion. You win both your ante and your call bet if your hand is higher than the dealer's. If the dealer's hand is higher, you lose both bets. There is a bonus payout schedule for winning hands, which makes Caribbean Stud more exciting:

- one pair pays 1 to 1
- two pair pays 2 to 1
- three-of-a-kind pays 3 to 1
- straight pays 4 to 1
- flush pays 5 to 1
- full house pays 7 to 1
- four-of-a-kind pays 20 to 1
- straight flush pays 50 to 1
- royal flush pays 100 to 1

The dealer must qualify and you must win the hand in order to receive a bonus payout.

The real attraction of Caribbean Stud is the chance to win big by hitting the progressive jackpot. This bet is purely optional on your part. To be eligible for winning all or part of this jackpot, you must wager an additional

$1. There is a drop slot for this bet directly in front of your position on the table. The progressive jackpot pay-offs are as follows.

- flush pays $50
- full house pays $75
- four-of-a-kind pays $100
- straight flush pays 10% of the progressive jackpot
- royal flush pays 100% of the progressive jackpot

Jackpots are paid regardless of whether the dealer's hand qualifies. Payoffs on the straight flush and royal flush are aggregate (if two or more players win on the same hand, the jackpot is divided proportionately).

Most gaming experts agree that betting the extra $1 for this wager is not a wise idea, even if the progressive jackpot gets up to $200,000. The odds of drawing a royal flush on your first five cards are 649,739 to 1. Using a computer, I figured out that if you played Caribbean Stud for eight hours a day, it would take you seven years, five months, and two days to play that many hands...which is about how long it took me to learn how to use a computer.

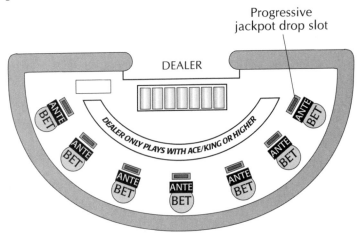

Progressive
jackpot drop slot

DEALER

DEALER ONLY PLAYS WITH ACE/KING OR HIGHER

ANTE BET

*Caribbean Stud table layout*

The biggest drawback to Caribbean Stud is that the dealer must qualify by having at least an ace and a king. You might have a great hand, but if the dealer doesn't qualify, all you'll win is your original ante. The house edge at Caribbean Stud is about 5.3% when played with optimum strategy.

Don't let the dealer's up card scare you out of the game. Many novice players will fold when the dealer exposes a good card, but the dealer may flip over four bad cards, and you've thrown in a winning hand. Also keep in mind that you cannot bluff in Caribbean Stud. If the dealer does qualify, it means he has a good hand. And he will qualify often enough that you shouldn't risk the call unless you have a good hand yourself.

## Basic Strategy

The optimum strategy for Caribbean Stud might be the easiest to remember of any game that requires hand evaluation. Gambling-math gurus Peter Griffin and John Gwynn Jr. have determined that you should call the dealer if your five-card hand is ace-king-jack-8-3 or better, and fold otherwise. That's all there is to it. For more information, read *Expert Strategy for Caribbean Stud Poker* by E.A. Frome and I.D. Frome, or *Mastering the Game of Caribbean Stud Poker* by Stanley Ko.

# Let It Ride

This game, introduced in Nevada casinos in 1993, has become such a favorite that it can now be played in more than 150 casinos throughout the world. What makes Let It Ride unique is that you can actually take back some of your money as the cards are being dealt. Invented by a company called Shuffle Master, Let It Ride is based on poker. And there's a special twist—for an extra $1, you are eligible for a side jackpot, which amounts to $20,000 for a royal flush. It also gives you a chance to win million-dollar grand prizes in the Let It Ride tournament. More about that later, but first let's look at how Let It Ride is played.

Each player makes three equal bets, one in each of three betting circles at each seat at the table. The dealer then deals three cards to each player face down. He also deals two "community" cards face down in front of himself.

Now, as the brochure says, it's time to have some fun. Take a look at your three cards. If you think you

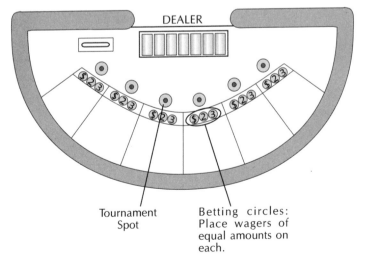

Tournament Spot

Betting circles: Place wagers of equal amounts on each.

*Let It Ride table layout*

have the beginnings of a good hand, or if you're just feeling lucky, then Let It Ride! If you're not pleased, signal the dealer and you can take back your first bet.

The dealer then turns over the first community card, which becomes the fourth card in your hand. Again, if you think you have a good hand, Let It Ride! If not, signal the dealer and take back your second bet. I told you this game was different.

Finally, the dealer turns over the second community card, completing your hand. If you've pulled back your first two bets, the third bet has to play. If your five-card hand contains a pair of 10s or better, you win. And you can win big bucks, as you can see by the payout table:

- pair of 10s or better pays even money
- two pair pays 2 to 1
- three-of-a-kind pays 3 to 1
- straight pays 5 to 1
- flush pays 8 to 1
- full house pays 11 to 1
- four-of-a-kind pays 50 to 1
- straight flush pays 200 to 1
- royal flush pays 1,000 to 1

Payouts on the royal flush are aggregate (if two or more players win on the same hand, the jackpot is divided proportionately).

## Tournament Jackpot

The specially designed Let It Ride layouts feature illuminated betting spots which allow you to participate in special payoffs when you make a straight or better. This is called the tournament spot, and it costs you an extra $1 per hand to play. All payouts are in addition to the regular Let It Ride awards, and are paid immediately.

- straight pays $20
- flush pays $50
- full house pays $75
- four-of-a-kind pays $200
- straight flush pays $2,000
- royal flush pays $20,000

The shot at the big payoff makes it tempting to bet that extra dollar, and to make it even more enticing there's an additional incentive. With any royal flush or straight flush, you earn an entry into the Let It Ride playoffs at a Nevada host casino, where you have a chance to make some really big money.

All playoff participants receive a round-one buy-in of $2,000 in non-negotiable chips. At the end of this round, the six finalists get the following cash awards:

Sixth place ................... $25,000
Fifth place................... $50,000
Fourth place ............... $75,000
Third place ................. $100,000
Second place .............. $200,000
Grand Prize ................ $1 million

The house edge at Let It Ride is 3.5%. Ninety-three percent of the time you will be taking back your first bet, and 85% of the time you will be taking back your second bet. Your third bet is locked in. Expect to stay in the game with all three bets only about once every 16 hands.

When you take down one of your bets, wait for your turn to do so, then signal the dealer by scratching your cards on the felt like you do to take a hit in blackjack. (Never touch your money.) If you decide to Let It Ride, tuck your cards face down underneath one of your bets.

Staying in the game with all three bets is not advisable if you don't have at least a pair of 10s. Having three high cards isn't much better, unless you can use them in a straight flush or a royal.

One big reason for Let It Ride's soaring popularity is the fact that you can win a lot of money off a small bet. I recently saw a player bet $10 in each of the three betting circles, along with another $1 in the tournament circle. He was dealt two 9s, and let all three bets ride (contrary to the proper strategy). The first community card was another 9. Naturally, the player let all his bets ride again. The second community card was another 9! The player won $1,500 for his four-of-a-kind, plus another $200 for his tournament bet. So for an investment of $31 the player received a staggering $1,700. Not bad (but, of course, it doesn't happen very often).

My wife, my mother-in-law, and I tried playing Let It Ride at home one night. We started out with 15 chips each, and played until the chips were gone (20 minutes). In all this time, the biggest winner among the three of us was two pair. Payback: 2 to 1. House edge this particular evening: 100%.

# Casino War

Based on the childhood game of "war" or "battle," casino war is now being offered in some Las Vegas casinos. There's not much to it, but that's the attraction of the game. Anybody who knows how to count can play it.

The dealer deals each player one card face up. Then the dealer takes a card face up. If you beat the dealer, you win your bet. If the dealer beats you, you lose. The cards have the same rankings as in poker, with the ace being the highest card, followed by the king, queen, jack, etc.

In the event your card ties the dealer's card, you can either go to war with the dealer (by matching your original bet), or you can surrender (by forfeiting half your original bet). If you go to war, the dealer will burn three cards and give you another card. Then he will burn three more cards and take one for himself.

If your second card is higher than the dealer's second card, you win your original bet. If the dealer wins, then you lose both your bets. If your second card ties the dealer's second card, you win. The rub here is the dealer doesn't pay off the second bet you risk to go to war, which is how the house gets its edge.

There is also a tie bet you can make which pays 10 to 1. (The house edge on that particular bet is around 18%.) As for going to war with the dealer, do it if you decide to play this game. The casino's edge is 3.7% if you surrender, and only 2.9% if you go to war.

# Big Six

Also known as the wheel of fortune or the money wheel, the big six can be found in almost every casino in town. It's called the big six because there are six different payoffs.

Bets are made by placing your money on the layout in one of the boxes. These boxes correspond to the numbers on the wheel and indicate the payoff rates. There are 54 slots on the wheel:

23 — $1 spots
15 — $2 spots
8  — $5 spots
4  — $10 spots
2  — $20 spots
1  — joker spot
1  — casino spot

Bet $1 on the $1 spot and you get paid even money; bet $1 on the $2 spot and get paid 2 to 1; bet $1 on the $5 spot and get paid 5 to 1; and so on. Bet the joker or casino spots (separately) and get paid 40 to 1.

The house edge on the big six is 14.8% on the $1 bets, and 24% on the joker or casino bets. Well, think about it. If there are 54 slots on the wheel, shouldn't a $1 bet on the joker pay 53 to 1? (Paging Mr. Barnum, Mr. P. T. Barnum...)

It's fun to watch, though. The next time you are suffering from an inferiority complex, just stand back and watch everyone at a big six wheel throw their money away. Suddenly you'll have a superiority complex.

Here's a funny story from one of my other books. A down-and-out dealer was hired to run the big six wheel in a downtown casino. While reviewing his profit-and-loss statement one morning, the casino manager noticed that the wheel was holding 100%! In other words, no one won anything. This went on for several weeks. The casino manager decided to watch the game and see why the casino was having such an incredible winning streak.

The dealer would wait until everyone placed their wagers, then stop the wheel (with his finger) on a losing number. Aghast, the casino manager called the dealer into his office and demanded an explanation.

"Well," the dealer replied, "you were nice enough to give me a job when I needed one. This is just my way of saying thanks."

# Race and Sports Books

Every major casino in Las Vegas has a race and sports book. The thinking is that people who gamble at blackjack and slot machines will probably gamble on sporting events and horse races as well. After all, everyone has a favorite team, or a favorite boxer, or a favorite nag, and here's your chance to put up or shut up. If nothing else, a sports book is a great place to settle down for a couple of hours and get yourself out of that "casino mode." Watch your favorite sporting event on a giant TV screen while enjoying a beer and sandwich from the nearby snack bar. At the Las Vegas Hilton Superbook, you can even get a free continental breakfast between 8:30 and 10 on weekday mornings.

In a race book you can bet on horse racing, harness racing, and greyhound racing —and in a sports book you can bet on football, basketball, baseball, boxing, hockey, auto racing, tennis, major golf tournaments, or even the Olympics. To keep you posted on your favorite sport, computer-generated betting information is updated in less than half a second on overhead electronic panels. It's not quite the same as picking up the phone and call-

**CASINO SECRET** In some casinos, you can set up a credit line at the sports book. Then simply call an assigned number to make your bets (it's illegal to gamble across state lines, so calls must be made inside the state of Nevada). Otherwise, casinos are restricted by law from connecting you to any sports book by telephone. You are also not allowed to use a cellular phone inside a sports book. Most sports books that allow phone betting require a minimum deposit of at least $350 and bets must be at least $50.

ing your neighborhood bookie—in Vegas, you've gotta pay before you bet.

The sports book makes its money on any game with a pointspread by charging bettors a 10% vigorish on each ticket. So if you make a $20 bet on your favorite team, you'll have to wager $22 to win $20. This gives the house an edge of about 5%.

Professional football is the most popular sport with bettors. College football is number two, followed by baseball, pro basketball, and college basketball. If it weren't for these four sports, the Hilton Superbook would probably be called the Hilton SuperCarWash.

The most popular bet is taking or laying the point spread. Example: Dallas is favored over Buffalo by six points. To bet Dallas, you would have to take Dallas at minus six (-6). So the score is actually Buffalo 6, Dallas 0 before the game even starts. Therefore, if Dallas wins by only five points, you lose your bet. If Dallas wins by six, you push and your money is returned to you. If Dallas wins by more than six points, you win.

You can also make what is called an "over" or "under" bet. The sports book will post a point total that the final combined score will either be over or under and you can bet either way.

Other popular bets include parlays and teasers, where you combine your wager on two games or more. Teasers pay less because of a softer pointspread, so most bettors prefer parlays. Your success with these types of bets depends on the outcome of multiple games on your ticket, and if you lose one game then the entire parlay is lost. A popular bet is to take the pointspread on your favorite team parlayed with either the "over" or "under." Parlays pay more than straight bets, but because you need more than one bet to win, they come in less often.

In baseball, a money line is used instead of a pointspread. If a team is a 7-5 favorite, you would have to bet $70 to win $50. It won't read that way on the board, though. It will read: "New York -140." Translation: New York is favored, and you have to bet $140 to win $100, the same ratio as $70 to win $50, or $7 to win $5.

To give yourself a better chance of winning at any game, study the teams. Is anybody hurt? Is your team playing at home or on the road? On grass or artificial turf? What's the weather like? Who won the last time they played each other? Former football coach Carmen Cozza once said, "A couple of unexpected injuries and people who don't come through as expected and the whole season can turn around."

That makes sense, but I'm still betting on the Chicago Cubs to win the pennant.

**CASINO SECRET** Get your best food bargains in the race and sports book. The snack bars are good and cheap, some casinos lay out free spreads for bettors, and during special promotions or events you're liable to find hot dogs and beer for as little as 25¢.

# Bingo

Who among us has not thrilled to these magical words?

"B-14." "N-42." "O-71."

Yes, it's bingo, one of the country's oldest games of chance, and also one of the most exasperating. You only need one more number and you'll finally win something after all these years, and then—from somewhere across the room—you hear the sickening sound of someone else screaming, "BINGO!!"

Bingo has its following of faithful fans, though. In fact, the Nevada Gaming Control Board determined in a recent statistical analysis that bingo offers the best return of any casino game, often paying back more than it takes in. Most game cards start at $1 and run to $6 and higher. You can play multiple boards, and you can play different denominations on each one.

In Las Vegas bingo is offered at more than a dozen casinos—Arizona Charlie's, Binion's Horseshoe, Boulder Station, Fiesta, Gold Coast, Gold Spike, Jerry's Nugget, Maxim, Palace Station, Sam's Town, Santa Fe, Showboat, Sunset Station, Texas Station, and Western among them. (Check each casino for times.)

Bingo in Las Vegas hardly compares with the games you play back home in the church basement. There's usually a $1,000 guaranteed payoff on any coverall, and at some casinos, such as the Horseshoe, you can win as much as $25,000. During special promotions around town, you might even win a brand new car.

Sessions are staggered, with a usual two-hour interval between games. And why do you think there's a two-hour wait? One casino boss explained it in these words. "Bingo is a leader. Most casinos lose money on bingo, but now they've got you where they want you. You're in the casino, and you've got to wait two hours to play again." So you can either go home and then come back, or you can kill some time at the slot machines. Starting to get the picture?

# Keno

Keno has been around for 3,000 years, only it wasn't always called keno. It started out as the Chinese lottery, and immigrants from the Orient brought it to this country back when the railroads were being built. Then it became lotto, and after that it was a form of bingo featured at traveling carnivals. In the 1930s it turned up as screeno, a game played in movie theaters during intermissions.

Reno gambler Warren Nelson liked the game and decided to put one in his casino. This created a problem, however. The game was definitely a lottery, and for some reason, lotteries aren't legal in the state of Nevada. (Well, we know what the reason is; the casinos don't want any outside competition.) So Nelson called his game racehorse keno, using the names of then-famous race horses along with the actual numbers. When off-track betting came under scrutiny in 1951, the name was changed to keno and it has been a casino staple ever since.

To play keno, just pick up a blank keno ticket at the casino keno lounge. Tickets are usually available in the hotel restaurants and coffee shops, too. In fact, many people like to play keno while they wait an hour and a half for their food to arrive. On each ticket, there are 80 numbers: 1 to 40 on the top half, and 41 to 80 on the bottom half. Simply X out any amount of numbers from one up to a maximum of 20, and if your numbers come up in the next game, you win.

Twenty of the 80 numbers are randomly drawn in each game and displayed on lighted keno boards positioned throughout the casino. About the only place you can't find a keno board is in the hotel bathrooms, so if nature calls be sure to give the keno attendant your cellular telephone number.

The excitement of keno lies in the thousands of possible number combinations that may be played during each game, and the outside chance of winning the top prize of $50,000 (or more). You can play in the relaxed atmosphere of the keno lounge, or you can buy your tickets from keno runners who flit through the casino like butterflies. They will even check your tickets to see if you won anything.

Keno is one of the biggest moneymakers in the casino. Not for you, unfortunately, but for the casino. Trying to hit eight numbers out of 20 numbers from a batch of 80 numbers sounds simple enough, but the odds of doing this are nearly a quarter of a million to one. Compared with this figure, winning $50,000 doesn't seem like very much, does it? As far as picking 20 out of 20 numbers, forget it! One statistician says you could play the same 20 numbers 24 hours a day, seven days a week, for eight generations of your family—and still never catch all 20 numbers on a keno ticket. By the time you win $50,000, it'll be worth just about enough to buy a loaf of bread.

But like Megabucks and those progressive jackpots on Let It Ride and Caribbean Stud, you have a chance of winning a lot of money off a small bet, and that's what gambling is all about.

### Straight Tickets

The most popular keno ticket is the straight ticket, where you bet straight up on any combination of one to 20 numbers. Most beginners prefer this ticket, because it's simple and you don't need a calculator to figure out the payoffs. In fact, there are rate cards in each keno lounge that have the pay tables written down for you. On the next page is one from the Horseshoe (check minimum bets and payoffs before you play; they vary in each casino).

## Mark Any 1 Number

| Catch | Bet 1.00 | Bet 2.00 | Bet 5.00 |
|---|---|---|---|
| 1 | 3.00 | 6.00 | 15.00 |

## Mark Any 2 Numbers

| Catch | Bet 1.00 | Bet 2.00 | Bet 5.00 |
|---|---|---|---|
| 2 | 12.00 | 24.00 | 60.00 |

## Mark Any 3 Numbers

| Catch | Bet 1.00 | Bet 2.00 | Bet 5.00 |
|---|---|---|---|
| 3 | 42.00 | 84.00 | 210.00 |
| 2 | 1.00 | 2.00 | 5.00 |

## Mark Any 4 Numbers

| Catch | Bet 1.00 | Bet 2.00 | Bet 5.00 |
|---|---|---|---|
| 4 | 125.00 | 250.00 | 625.00 |
| 3 | 3.00 | 6.00 | 15.00 |
| 2 | 1.00 | 2.00 | 5.00 |

## Mark Any 5 Numbers

| Catch | Bet 1.00 | Bet 2.00 | Bet 5.00 |
|---|---|---|---|
| 5 | 750.00 | 1,500.00 | 3,750.00 |
| 4 | 13.00 | 26.00 | 65.00 |
| 3 | 1.00 | 2.00 | 5.00 |

## Mark Any 6 Numbers

| Catch | Bet 1.00 | Bet 2.00 | Bet 5.00 |
|---|---|---|---|
| 6 | 1,495.00 | 2,990.00 | 7,475.00 |
| 5 | 93.00 | 186.00 | 465.00 |
| 4 | 4.00 | 8.00 | 20.00 |
| 3 | 1.00 | 2.00 | 5.00 |

## Mark Any 7 Numbers

| Catch | Bet 1.00 | Bet 2.00 | Bet 5.00 |
|---|---|---|---|
| 7 | 8,000.00 | 16,000.00 | 40,000.00 |
| 6 | 420.00 | 840.00 | 2,100.00 |
| 5 | 20.00 | 40.00 | 100.00 |
| 4 | 1.00 | 2.00 | 5.00 |

## Mark Any 8 Numbers

| Catch | Bet 1.00 | Bet 2.00 | Bet 5.00 |
|---|---|---|---|
| 8 | 25,000.00 | 50,000.00 | 50,000.00 |
| 7 | 1,495.00 | 2,990.00 | 7,475.00 |
| 6 | 90.00 | 180.00 | 450.00 |
| 5 | 9.00 | 18.00 | 45.00 |

As you can see, missing by just one number can mean a big difference in your payoff. The fewer numbers you bet, the less you can win, so it's very tempting to go for the big money by betting eight numbers, or an "eight spot" as it's called. Remember the odds, though, and the fact that you have to catch around half your numbers just to get your money back.

*straight ticket*

## Split Tickets

This type of ticket allows you to write two or more tickets in one, by splitting your numbers into different groups. For instance, you can bet six numbers in one group and six numbers in another group. Or you can bet eight numbers in one group, four in another, and four in a third. All groupings of the same number of spots must be for the same amount of money. Payoffs are the same as on regular straight tickets. Circle your groups, or draw a line between the groups you've marked. Keep in mind, though, that a number in one group cannot be used in another.

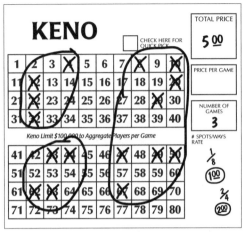

*split ticket*

## Way Tickets

This type of ticket must have at least three groups of equal amounts of numbers. The advantage of a way ticket over a split ticket is that you win if you catch numbers in any of your groupings, whereas with a split ticket each grouping is a separate bet. The disadvantage is that it raises the cost of the ticket.

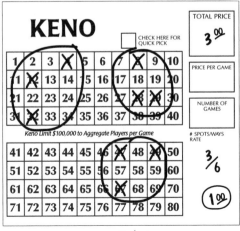

*way ticket*

## Combination Tickets

A combination ticket is a way ticket that went to college. More complicated than other tickets, it's popular because you can use combinations to make a greater variety of bets. You can bet on equal groups of numbers; you can bet on unequal groups of numbers; or you can combine the groups into all sorts of combinations. For example, pick 12 numbers. Using a combination ticket, you could combine these 12 numbers into three four spots, three eight spots, and one 12-spot.

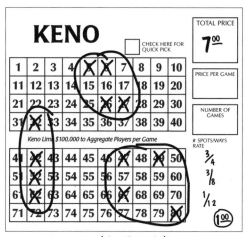

*combination ticket*

## King Tickets

Circle one number on your keno ticket. This becomes your king number, which is used with the other numbers you pick to make a fancy combination ticket. For example, circle 23. Mark two other groupings of four numbers each. With a king ticket, you now have two five spots and one nine spot.

*king ticket*

## Basic Strategy

The house edge at keno is around 30%, but there are a few strategies you can use to give yourself a better chance of winning.

You can shop around for better returns, but most people don't want to be bothered with that. Independent comparisons that I've seen seem to consistently put the Gold Coast at the top of the keno-payout rankings. Another casino that often appears near the top is the Frontier. And downtown casinos seem to outpay those on the Strip.

There's a case for playing only one spots. The casino edge is a little lower (almost always 25%), and a single number will come in most often. The payoff on a winning one spot, though, is only 3-for-1, so you lose the excitement generated by the possibility of the big score.

My personal preference is to avoid betting less than five numbers on a game. Refer back to our Horseshoe keno ticket and you'll see why. Catch all your numbers on a $5 four-spot and you win $625. Catch all your numbers on a $5 five-spot and you win $3,750. Big difference. If I get lucky, I want to win something substantial.

If you want to chase a really big score, you can look around for keno games with big progressive meters. The Gold Coast has a famous $5 eight-spot that actually has no house advantage when the meter rises above $430,000.

Other advice from the experts:

• Don't bet serious money at keno. As far as casino games go, it's the slowest horse in the race. You're betting on a long shot.
• Play downtown. Tickets are cheaper.
• Stick with the same numbers. It won't improve your chances, but nothing is more frustrating than changing your numbers, then seeing all your old numbers pop up one after the other.

When all else fails, you might try playing keno the way I do. Mark your numbers, get your ticket validated, then kneel in front of the keno board and recite the following:

"Our Father, who art in heaven, hallowed be Thy name ... "

# 9
# Comps
# and Other Goodies

Now that you know how to play the games, the next questions is, how do you get all those casino perks that go hand in hand with gambling? You may have heard that casino complimentaries (known as "comps") are available everywhere. And they are. But only if you know how to work the system. They won't just come to you. And I can tell you that most people don't get nearly as many comps as they could.

Whole books have been written in recent years that tell you how to take advantage of the comp system (*Comp City* and *The Las Vegas Advisor Guide to Slot Clubs*, both published by Huntington Press, to be specific). If you study them and apply the techniques that they lay out, you'll do just fine. But from my point of view, no matter how good you get at reeling in comps, it definitely ain't like it was in the old days.

The reason is simple. Corporations own Las Vegas today. And corporations do business much differently than in the free-for-all times when "family-owned" casinos ran the show. In those days, you knew you wouldn't win much. How could you, when table limits were $500 and slot jackpots were $100? The truth was that you would probably lose all the money you brought with you, but you were sure to have a good time and get a few freebies in the process.

Want a meal? No problem. Want to see a show? Sure, why not. No money to get home? Here's a bus ticket. Need more credit? We'll call your bank in the morning and have them wire some more money to your casino account. In the meantime, here's a free room for the night.

People loved it. Sure, they went broke, but what great stories they had to tell when they got back home. They told their friends, and their friends told *their* friends, and all of them headed for Sin City, USA.

Corporations, however, have a different way of doing business. Corporations expect each department to show a profit. Corporations want all of your money, but corporations don't want to give any of it back—not even in the form of complimentary services. Corporations don't seem to understand the concept on which Las Vegas was founded. The casino industry is a people business, and customer service is the only service a casino provides.

Therefore, if you lose all your dough at the dice tables and ask for a free meal in the coffee shop, it creates a problem for the corporation's bookkeepers. The casino is making money, but now the coffee shop isn't showing a profit. Thus begins a chain reaction that eventually carries over to every other department in the hotel: rooms and reservations, showroom, lounges, restaurants, bars, gift shops, even the cabanas by the swimming pool.

A perfect example of this is the way you get cigarettes in a casino today. Before Howard Hughes bought his first casino and started a stampede by other corporate conglomerates, cigarettes were free. Boxes of them sat on every table game in the casino and you could grab as many as you wanted. After the corporations took over, the cigarettes were kept in locked drawers. If a player wanted some smokes he had to ask for them, and the pit boss decided if his play warranted a free pack. Now it's even worse. Cigarettes are supplied by concessionaires, who pay the casino for this privilege. If a player wants a pack of cigarettes today he tells the dealer, who tells the supervisor, who tells the pit clerk, who calls the cigarette girl, who gets an order form signed by the supervisor. By the time a customer gets his cigarettes, he has practically kicked the habit.

Cocktails are still free, because there is no more sure-fire way to loosen a gambler's inhibitions than by getting him plastered. Today, however, most casino supervisors have to undergo alcohol-awareness training to detect people who have over-imbibed. If the supervisor thinks you've had too much to drink, you won't get any more. This is to protect the casino against lawsuits from sore losers, so if you can't walk in a straight line, at least try to *stand* in a straight line.

One of the great ironies of casino life is that the player who can get a comp usually doesn't need one, and the person who needs a comp can't afford one. A veteran pit boss once told me: "If you've got enough money, you can get anything in Las Vegas that you want." Well, that's fine, but if you're just trying to get something free from the casino, you usually have to prove that you deserve it. That means you have to gamble, and in the long run it would often be cheaper just to pay for it. Fact is, though, if you're going to gamble anyway, you might as well get back whatever they'll give you. In a bit I'll pass on some comp secrets, but first let me show you how comps work in modern-day Las Vegas.

Comps are based on three factors: your average bet, the casino advantage at the game you play, and how long you play. These three numbers are multiplied by each other to calculate the casino's "theoretical win." Generally, the casino is willing to give back 25% to 40% of that amount in comps.

If you play for an hour, betting between $10 and $25 a hand, you can usually qualify for a free meal at the hotel buffet. The casino figures you will lose much more than the price of that $10 buffet.

A $25 to $50 minimum bet over a four-hour period will usually get you a casino rate on your room, which is about half the regular price.

A $75 to $100 minimum bet over a four-hour period usually gets you a free room.

A $125 to $150 minimum bet over a four-hour period can earn you free room, food, and beverages (or "RF&B" as it's called in casino jargon).

An average bet of $150 to $500 over four hours will earn you a free room, gourmet meals, room service, and possibly a round-trip plane ticket between your hometown and Las Vegas.

An average bet of $500 or more over four hours will usually get you ANYTHING YOU WANT! A limo with your own driver at your disposal, a private chef, a private casino to play in, unlimited use of the spa and health club, golf on any course in Las Vegas, a celebrity suite overlooking the pool, casino gifts in your room, your own private tour of the Grand Canyon, even the company jet to whisk you and your friends off to Lake Tahoe or Disneyland.

Herb Wolff is a high roller from Atlantic City. He makes no bones about it. In fact, his wife Phyllis wrote a book about their experiences called *Lifestyles of a High Roller*. Over the years, the casinos they visit have lavished them with such gifts as a Gucci watch, luggage, a Waterford crystal lamp, a gold clock, Rosenthal china and glasses, a silver serving tray, leather accessories, a gold picture frame, and all kinds of toiletries.

Each time the Wolffs check into their suite, some nice little present awaits: flower assortments, fruit baskets, stocked refrigerator, T-shirts, tote bags, sunglasses, hats, beach towels, a crystal wine decanter, a gold pen and pencil set, stuffed toy animals for the grandchildren, sweatshirts, jackets with the hotel logo, and on one occasion, a baseball autographed by Willie Mays. How do they get all these things home? Why, in their own private limousine that takes them from the casino in Atlantic City right to their doorstep in New York City.

We can't all qualify for the type of treatment the Wolffs receive, but there are things you can do to start earning your wings in the comp system.

• Get rated. Before you play any of the games, give your name to the floor supervisor in charge of your table. At the slot machines, give your name to the slot supervisor. Make sure you always get credit for your play, regardless of how much you bet. The supervisor will monitor the length of time you play and the size of your bets. If you move to a different table or a different row of machines, be sure to alert the new supervisor. This is important, because if you ask for something, it helps a lot if someone knows who you are.

• Don't split your gaming budget between casinos. This minimizes the amount of time you spend gambling in each one, which decreases the amount each casino will give you back. Where you stay is where you should play.

• Remember that smaller casinos work on a lower profit margin, so it's usually easier to get comps in a large resort. There was one small casino in town (now closed) where only the casino manager could issue comps. A man at the dice table asked for a free meal in the buffet. The casino manager studied the man's rating slip, then said to him, "Okay, I'll give you a buffet comp. But you can't eat any meat."

### Free Meals

If you're gambling, even for low stakes, your chances of getting a comp for a meal are pretty good as long as you're not afraid to ask, and you don't ask for too much when you do.

The supervisor has to justify any comps that he gives out. He can get in trouble by indiscriminately issuing comps, so he will usually stick to the guidelines outlined earlier. However, most casinos are not as strict with the buffet or coffee shop as they are with the production show and gourmet restaurant. The supervisor knows this, so there is a good chance of getting a comp for one of these meals. Here's how. After playing for a while, catch the eye of a supervisor at one of the tables and wait for him to approach you. It may take a minute or two, because he has a lot of things to do. When he comes over, give him a warm smile. Shake hands with him. Then tell him that you've been playing for a couple of hours and would like to get something to eat. If he likes you (or your play actually warrants it), he might just issue the comp on the spot. It's more likely, though, that he'll tell you you need to play a little longer. That's okay. Just ask him how much longer, then decide whether it's worth it or not.

If the supervisor asks where you want to eat, tell him the coffee shop. He may not comp you to the coffee shop, but nine times out of ten you'll at least get the buffet. The quality won't be as high, but somehow it always tastes better when it's free. One pit boss told me, "If somebody has enough guts to ask me for a comp, I will always give him the buffet because it's cheap. You have to be careful with the restaurants. Four people could run up a $200 bill in the coffee shop." He told of one person whose food check was $138, and $32 of that was for imported chocolate milk!

As far as gourmet restaurants are concerned, I wouldn't even bother trying to get comped to one. For one thing, it's almost impossible unless you're a bona fide high roller. Secondly, the tip will cost you more than the entire bill for eating at a regular restaurant, since the waiters will try to run up the tab as high as they can (the bigger the bill, the bigger the tip). That's why I'm not that crazy about eating in gourmet restaurants. I say that if there are more than two forks next to your plate, the meal will definitely cost too much—even if you get it free.

If a boss seems a little skeptical of your claim of having played for a while, it's probably because lots of people try to abuse the comp system. There was one man who approached a pit boss with the following story.

"Hello, I'm Diana Ross's hairdresser, and I was eating in the buffet when Diana called and wanted her hair done for the show tonight. I told the girl in the buffet that I would be back in about an hour to finish my meal, and she said it wouldn't be a problem. But when I came back, she had gone off duty and the new girl wouldn't let me back in. Now, I'm not asking for a comp or anything. I just want to get what I paid for, and I already paid for the buffet."

This story actually worked the first time the man used it. Unfortunately, he tried it again the next time Diana Ross was in town, and as luck would have it, he used it on the same boss who gave him the first comp. Needless to say, he didn't get the second one.

Just remember that you have to ask. A friend of mine likes to say that "the squeaky wheel gets the greasy breakfast comp."

### Free Drinks

Getting a free drink in a casino is a fairly easy matter. For one thing, as long as you're gambling, your drinks are complimentary. You can get as many as you want. And if you give the cocktail waitress a $5 tip, she'll be at your side every time you look up. Stiff her for your drink, and you might have to wait until the end of the shift when a new waitress comes on duty to get another one. Back in the rip-roaring days of early Las Vegas, some cocktail waitresses would "special" your next drink if you didn't tip. A special was a shot of vodka added to whatever you were drinking. Bourbon and coke? Shot of vodka in it. Whiskey sour? Shot of vodka in it. A couple of these and they mailed you home in an envelope.

It's funny how some people will try to get a drink without tipping. As soon as the cocktail waitress arrives with a person's drink, he suddenly becomes engrossed in the game he is playing. Other popular ways to avoid tipping include the following time-worn phrases:

"I don't have any change right now."

"I'll catch you later."

And: "Thank you."

One cocktail waitress told me she gets plenty of $3 tips from Asian customers. After she brings their drinks, many Asians will ask how much they owe her. When she replies that the drink is free, they think she is saying "three," and give her $3.

Cocktail waitresses must pay taxes on each drink they serve, whether they get a tip or not. Otherwise, they are not in compliance with IRS tax regulations. This tax can be as high as 30% of the retail price for each cocktail. So if you order a $2 frozen daiquiri from a cocktail waitress, she might have to pay as much as 60¢ in taxes on it. If you don't tip her, you're costing her not only time but money as well. So now that I've seen to it that every cocktail waitress in the world will buy this book, I can move on to other matters.

Each casino has its share of cocktail lounges. After a long tiring day of eating free meals, you might want to enjoy a free drink in the lounge. Use the same techniques that you used to get a free meal, but ask for a drink instead. Most supervisors are fairly lenient about comping drinks in the lounge. It isn't costing the casino that much,

**CASINO SECRET**

While gambling, ask for liquor by name brand, or ask for bottled beer. Otherwise, you'll get house booze, which is usually the cheapest stuff the casino can buy.

and they write it off anyway. What's nice about it from your standpoint is that many lounges feature good entertainment, so you get to see a free show while you're having a free drink.

You will usually see an "L" and "U" printed on the comp slip. The L stands for limited, the U stands for unlimited. Your slip will probably have the L marked, which means you can order anything within reason. Don't ask for a bottle of chilled Cabernet Sauvignon. First of all, it's too expensive, and secondly, nobody drinks Cabernet chilled.

### Souvenirs

You always hear the same thing when you tell your friends you're going to Las Vegas. "Bring me back a souvenir." Well, those souvenirs can get expensive. A dice clock, for example, will set you back around $40. You can also get casino-chip money clips, dice rosary beads, roulette-wheel ashtrays, chocolate casino chips, toy slot machines, postcards with your name in lights on a hotel marquee...all kinds of great little items that your friends will treasure always, or at least until you leave their house.

No one wants a roulette-wheel ashtray. No one wants a dice clock. No one wants a T-shirt that reads "I Lost My Ass In Las Vegas." What they really want is money! But since you're not going to give them any, how about the next best thing? Why not give them a little piece of real Las Vegas history? Give them a deck of playing cards that were once used on a real blackjack table, or a pair of dice that came right off a Vegas crap game.

Some casinos in Nevada still give cards and dice away. Just ask a supervisor for a souvenir deck of cards or "some souvenir dice." Don't ask for a *pair* of dice; you might only get two. My way, you might get a handful. Some people have a big sob story all rehearsed. A son is in the hospital and some dice from his favorite casino would mean so much. The church is having a Las Vegas night, or the retirement home needs cards. Don't bother! Just ask for the stuff.

Some casinos won't give away playing cards, purely because of economics. Cards are usually dealt from multiple-deck shoes, and it takes hours of manpower to sort the cards back into individual decks. If this is the case in your casino, just buy a few packs at the gift shop. They're cheap and they make great gifts. On the other hand, free dice are usually easy to get.

Speaking of dice, the ones from Las Vegas make wonderful little conversation pieces. Dice are changed in casinos at the end of each eight-hour shift. Each die has the casino logo on it, and each one is numbered, usually on the 6-spot. At Caesars Palace, each die has a small separation between the top of the "L" and the bottom of the "L" on the word "Palace." Look at the 4-spot, and you will see a small circle where the die has been "canceled." If you hold one of the dice from Caesars up to the light, you'll see a small "L" on the inside of the die.

These are precautions to safeguard the casino against cheaters. Personally, I have never seen anyone switch dice in a casino. That doesn't mean it wasn't done; it just means I never saw them do it.

## Line Passes

One of life's greatest disappointments is arriving at a casino restaurant or buffet, weak-kneed from hunger, only to discover a line of other starving people stretching halfway to the end of the building. In a case like this, you have three options. You can go to the end of the line and hope the restaurant doesn't run out of food before you get inside; you can go somewhere else; or you can get a line pass.

To get a line pass, simply approach a supervisor who saw you playing earlier and ask for one. People use all sorts of excuses to get a line pass (or pit pass, as it's sometimes called), but don't bother. A line pass does not cost the casino anything, so you have a better chance of getting it than you do other comps. Then just walk to the front of the line, present your line pass to the hostess, and in you go. Note: Refrain from looking at the other people in line as you whisk past them. You'll probably get some very dirty looks, or someone just might ask for your autograph. Only celebrities get service like this.

The following is a true story. A wealthy gambler who was accustomed to getting the finer things in life from his favorite casino got called away from the dice table one afternoon. His wife was ill, so he drove her to the hospital. Upon arriving at the hospital he found a long line of people waiting for treatment. He got on the phone and called the casino. "I need a line pass to the emergency room," he said.

## Coupons

Bargain hunters use coupons when they go to the grocery store. Bargain hunters use coupons when they go to Las Vegas. You can find coupons and two-for-one specials in casino funbooks, in local magazines and newspapers, and in handouts downtown and on the Strip. A lot of the smaller casinos offer them; it's their way of competing with the big boys. It's also their way of getting you to spend some of your own money after you've gone through the coupons.

By using coupons, you can get free novelties, free photographs, free sun visors, free drinks, free slot pulls, free rolls of nickels, free keno tickets, free plays at different table games, even a free spin on the casino money wheel. Or you can buy one show ticket and get one free. Buy one breakfast, get another free.

"You want coffee, toast, bacon, and hashbrowns with those eggs? Sorry, that's extra."

Aw, I'm just kidding. It's true that you can get a lot of great bargains by using coupons and two-for-one specials, and I recommend them when possible. Many give you good value for your money. But remember that these coupons are designed for one reason, and that's to get you inside the casino. Then it's up to you to get back out while you're still in one piece.

Of course, there will always be someone who can wring water out of a rock. Take the following couple who shared their vacation log with a local newspaper:

*Monday. Free breakfast, free bloody Marys, free popcorn. Got $2 in cash from funbooks. Found 5¢, played in machine, and lost it. Found one penny, added to bankroll. Free cocktails. Free slot pulls. Played free keno ticket, didn't win. Free cocktails. Dinner, two-for-one coupon. Free champagne and lounge show. Total cost for the day: 9¢.*

*Tuesday. Free breakfast, free bloody Marys, free popcorn. Got $2 in cash from funbooks. Free slot pulls, made $2.30. Found 5¢, made $1. Free hot dogs and champagne. Found 25¢, made $2. Hot dogs again. Tremendous strawberry shortcake for $1.50. Free lounge show. Free breakfast at 11 p.m. Tip 25¢. Total cost for the day: $3.55 profit.*

Does this seem like fun to you? I wouldn't even pick up a penny if I saw one on the floor, much less write it down in a daily log. And if I ate popcorn for breakfast, or champagne and hot dogs for lunch, I'd spend all my profits on stomach medicine. Still, some people really get a kick out of turning the tables on the casinos in this way. If you're one of them, just keep your eyes open and investigate every offer you come across.

### Rooms

Even though Las Vegas has more hotel rooms than any other major city in the world (more than 100,000 with more coming), it's still hard to get one during the weekends and busy times. Your best bet is to call the 800 number of your favorite Vegas hotel and make reservations well in advance.

The cost of rooms is still low, but expect to pay more than you used to. Las Vegas is changing horses in midstream again and going after a more affluent crowd. I know, this is supposed to be a family destination, but that approach isn't working out. Conventioneers and family vacationers don't gamble as much, so Vegas hotels have had to raise room rates to ensure profits. The Lady Luck, for example, has done a complete turnaround with its new advertising slogan: "Three days, two nights, and no kids!"

As far as the casinos are concerned, kids are a pain in the neck. They cry, they disrupt things, but most importantly, they don't gamble. Teenagers are even worse. They try to drink and they try to gamble. Consequently, casino personnel spend much of their time checking IDs, ever fearful that one of these baby-faced tourists will slip past them and get the hotel in a whole pack of trouble. The Las Vegas police department recently used a 19-year-old in an undercover operation to see if minors were being served alcohol or allowed to gamble. Apparently he got by in a few places. That's terrible, I know, but it's hard to fault the casinos. To me, *everyone* looks like they're 19!

At the Dunes, a young woman once shot the dice for nearly three hours. When the hand ended, everyone at the table had won thousands of dollars. Several of the players hoisted the young woman onto their shoulders and paraded her around the casino. A Dunes public relations man happened upon the scene and realized this would be a perfect opportunity to get some much-needed publicity for the hotel. Her picture was taken, and she was asked for her driver's license so that her name would be spelled correctly. It turned out the woman was only 19 years old! Needless to say, this is one story that didn't make the papers.

To pacify the younger generation, casinos have designed all kinds of special attractions: pinball arcades, water parks, amusement parks, theme parks. They have been a huge success. Not because the kids like them, but because the adults do! We are all kids at heart. That's what makes Las Vegas so much fun. The ideal tourists today are a couple in their forties, with about $4,000 in cash or credit cards and four days to spend it. This couple isn't looking for funbooks or 99¢ shrimp cocktails. They work hard, they play hard and they don't mind paying for what they get.

Thus they will pay $80 for a room, or $160 for a suite, which are now the average rates for good accommodations. Even at these prices, room rates are still lower than they are in New York or Chicago, but they're going up fast. Oh, you can still get a cheap room, but you won't be where the action is. If that isn't important to you, then stay at the Continental, Vacation Village, Showboat, Boulder Station, Palace Station, Gold Coast, Fiesta, Texas Station, Arizona Charlie's, Sam's Town, downtown, or Primm (at the California state line).

Want to go middle of the road? Stay at Circus Circus, Excalibur, Luxor, Imperial Palace, Bourbon Street, Aladdin, Sahara, Frontier, Riviera, Maxim, Stratosphere, Golden Nugget, Barbary Coast, Stardust, Debbie Reynolds, Harrah's, San Remo, Rio, Flamingo Hilton, Tropicana, Monte Carlo, or New York-New York.

If you want to go first class, then stay at Caesars Palace, Bally's, MGM Grand, Mirage, Treasure Island, Sheraton Desert Inn, Las Vegas Hilton, or Alexis Park.

Personally, I would rather stay in a smaller place and have extra money for other things. Ask yourself this question. How much time are you going to spend in your room? Still, it's a matter of personal taste. An old friend of mine lives in Texas, and his motto is, "If you can't go first class, then don't go at all." I haven't seen him in 27 years.

Times to avoid going to Las Vegas are on holidays or

during special events. Most people wouldn't go to New Orleans during Mardi Gras or Atlanta during the Olympics. Don't go to Las Vegas over Super Bowl weekend, during the Comdex convention, the National Finals Rodeo, the college basketball playoffs, over a long holiday weekend, or while a big boxing match is being held. At any given moment, there are more than 150,000 tourists in Las Vegas. During a special event, that figure is likely to double.

The best times to go to Las Vegas are during the week (rooms are cheaper), the month of June (graduations and weddings keep tourism down), the two weeks before Christmas, immediately *after* any holiday, and in spring and fall.

When in doubt, use a travel agent. Forty percent of Vegas tourists do. That way, if anything goes wrong, you've got someone else to blame.

### Shows

Here is a typical night's entertainment line-up in Las Vegas. George Carlin at Bally's, *Country Tonight* at the Aladdin, Julio Iglesias at Caesars Palace, Buddy Hackett at the Sheraton Desert Inn, *The Great Radio City Spectacular* at the Flamingo Hilton, *Starlight Express* at the Las Vegas Hilton, *Legends In Concert* at the Imperial Palace, Don Rickles at MGM Grand, *Siegfried & Roy* at the Mirage, *Splash* at the Riviera, *Enter The Night* at the Stardust, *Mystère* at Treasure Island, *Folies Bergere* at the Tropicana,

**CASINO SECRET**
It gets so hot in Las Vegas during June, July and August that tourism takes a nose dive. Look for hotel price wars in the summer, and keep calling 800 numbers until you find the best room rate in town.

circus acts at Circus Circus, *King Arthur's Tournament* at the Excalibur, and Debbie Reynolds at Debbie Reynolds.

Las Vegas is still the Entertainment Capital of the World. In fact, that used to be the city's slogan. You probably heard it yourself at one time or another, or saw it in a newspaper underneath a photo of some gorgeous Vegas showgirl. But someone decided that this slogan didn't do the town justice. So it became "Las Vegas, Gateway to the Great Southwest." And then it was "Las Vegas, the American Way to Play." And then it was...come to think about it, I don't think Las Vegas has a slogan now.

Oh well, it doesn't need one. What it needs is someone like me to tell you what to see once you get to Las Vegas and how much it'll cost you. So I will, "There's plenty to see and it'll cost you plenty."

The price of a Vegas show can range anywhere from $17.95 to $85 per person. That's just to get in. If you want a good seat, figure on spending another $10 to $20 either for a "VIP" seat or for the captain (more on this later). Let me emphasize that many shows in Las Vegas are now handled by Ticketron and other automated ticket agencies. Your seats are assigned to you, and you're usually stuck with them. There's no one to whom you can complain except a bored ticket-taker who's mad anyway because she's working and you're not.

Anything can happen on a big night out in Vegas, as you're about to find out in this true story of an experience my wife and I had. I call it "Binocular Heaven." Henry, would you dim the lights, please?

### Binocular Heaven

It was a once-in-a-lifetime rock 'n' roll treat, a chance to see the Rolling Stones. Of all the rock groups down through the ages, they were right up there with the Beatles—maybe not as pure, maybe not as sweet. Still, there was a kind of sexual defiance about them that made you hate them and love them at the same time.

At first, all we heard were the rumors. The Rolling Stones might be coming to Vegas. They might be playing on the grounds of the old Dunes. They might be at the Silver Bowl or at the Thomas & Mack Arena. Then without so much as a down-and-dirty in-your-face steel guitar riff, there appeared a full-page ad in the *Review-Journal*. The Rolling Stones were coming to the MGM Grand Garden Arena, two shows only, tickets to go on sale the following Monday starting at 8 a.m. You could stand in line or call on the phone. Either way, it was first come, first served.

The tickets were way out of line: $100, $200, $300. But for my wife and me the price wasn't that important. It was our seventh wedding anniversary, and this would be our gift to one another. She would pay for my $100 ticket; I would pay for hers. It still came out of the same pot, but it seemed cheaper that way.

The Stones were getting up there. Mick Jagger and Keith Richards were 51; Charlie Watts was 53. And the story making the rounds was that this would be their final tour. If we didn't see them now, we might never get the chance.

Monday morning at 8 o'clock I dialed the MGM. I got a busy signal. I tried again at 8:15. Busy signal. Nine o'clock. Busy signal. Nine-thirty. Busy signal. I called my wife. "You try," I told her. "I can't get through."

My wife, who has been lucky at everything in her life except for lotteries, slot machines, and possibly her choice of a husband, called me back half an hour later. "I got the tickets," she announced.

Hey, my baby came through again. Sure, $200 was a lot of money, but I had to remind myself that this was the concert of the year, these were the Rolling Stones, and there would never be another rock group that—

"They were two hundred dollars *each*."

Two hundred dollars each! Multiply $200 by two tickets and that comes to $400!! Actually, the total was $424 after they tacked on the handling charges and the sales tax.

Fast forward to Friday, October 14th. We arrive at the MGM Grand Garden entrance. Ticket scalpers give us a questioning look as we walk past. Business is bad. Scalpers always seem to get the good seats somehow, then they sell them for an outlandish profit. Not tonight. One scalper bought twelve $200 seats for this concert, and can only manage to sell eight of them at the same price he bought them for. Another scalper sacrifices a $300 seat for $70 right before showtime.

One of the highlights of attending a big concert is seeing celebrities in the audience. You've got to have a keen eye, though, because—

"Look, hon, there's Woody Harrelson."

"What? Where?"

Too late. I turn just in time to see a blonde-haired man in blue jeans round the corner and disappear. But I can tell you the following facts about Woody Harrelson now. He carries his wallet in his left back pocket and he has a tiny bald spot on the back of his head.

Outside the Grand Garden entrance a booth is set up where Rolling Stones merchandise is being sold at an almost frantic pace. Voodoo Lounge baseball caps are $22, T-shirts were $25 and $35, posters $10, programs $18, hooded sweatshirts $60, baseball shirts $90, bomber's jackets $150, and motorcycle jackets $450. They're adorned with skeletons, lips, and tongues. Lips? Tongues? I feel like a modern-day Rip Van Winkle, roused from sleep in the wrong century.

Suddenly the long lines of people waiting to get inside the Grand Garden come to a complete stop. There is some kind of bottleneck up ahead. I crane to see. Well, for crying out loud, metal detectors are positioned at the entrance. What do they think we're going to do—hijack the damn auditorium?

Now they're going through purses. Anyone with a

camera or tape recorder gets turned away. I whisper to my wife, "You didn't bring the camera, did you?"

"Yes. It's in my purse, right next to your tape recorder."

So we walk another 200 yards to a security station, where we stand in line to turn in our "contraband." Then we hike back to the entrance and finally find ourselves inside the cavernous Grand Garden. Music is already blasting from the stage, but it turns out to be a warmup act, a guy named Buddy Guy.

We find our seats: Row U, 15 and 16, Upper Plaza. From this vantage point, Buddy Guy is nothing more than a rumor. Fortunately, I have my binoculars, so I can almost make out Buddy's facial features. Fortunately, I also have earplugs. The music is deafening.

"CAN YOU SEE??" my wife screams in my ear.

"NO, I'M OKAY!!"

"*CAN — YOU — SEE??*"

"OH! YEAH! YEAH, I CAN SEE!!"

I can see, all right. I can see lots of empty chairs, down in the $300 seat section. I can see the $100 seats a lot better, because they're only about four rows back from where we're sitting in the $200 seats. I can see the stage, because suddenly the music stops and the lights go up. Workers rush to and fro. Silvery staircases slide into place. A giant screen appears.

It's the calm before the storm, and now the room starts to fill. There's a hum in the air as the minutes tick past. Then the lights dim and a solitary figure ambles onstage. A spotlight illuminates his face. It's Mick Jagger. With a mighty roar the crowd is on its feet.

The show is a kaleidoscope of sounds and colors. There are cones of fire, an inflatable 75-foot Elvis, a 92-foot serpent, a colossal TV screen that lets you see everything up close. Songs I didn't even know I remembered come surging up through my subconscious as the Rolling Stones sing them again: "Honky Tonk Woman,

Brown Sugar, Not Fade Away, Tumbling Dice, Miss You, Monkey Man, Beast of Burden, I Go Wild," and finally—

"I know it's only rock and roll, but I like it!"

One encore—"Jumpin' Jack Flash"—and then it was over. But during those two hours, and through 27 songs, time stood still in that big room. For a glimmer of a moment, I was a kid again and life was pure fun again.

Was it worth $424? I should say not. Would I do it again? In a second.

According to statistics, the average Vegas tourist allots $25 for entertainment and sightseeing combined. That's not a lot, so you have to make good choices. If I were going to Las Vegas for the first time, here's what I would do. I would plan on seeing one good show and eating in a couple of nice restaurants. Pinch pennies on other things if you want, but Vegas is famous for good food and good entertainment, so take advantage of it. Come on, you worked all year for this vacation, so live a little.

In Las Vegas, you need reservations for all shows and for most good restaurants. Make restaurant reservations in mid-afternoon. Make show reservations as early in the day as possible. To see performers who are usually sold out, book your room at the hotel where that star is performing. After high rollers, hotel guests are given priority for show reservations.

If there is a line waiting to get inside the showroom, get a line pass from a casino supervisor. If you don't want to bother, then arrive just before showtime. The lines are gone by then, and you can waltz right in.

"If I give the maître d' $20 to $40, or even $50, I know I'm going to get into any restaurant in town. I also know that I'm going to get any seat I want in the showroom." So says a long-time Vegas player.

This is the old adage in action. Money talks. In fact, in Las Vegas it practically shouts. "I went to a major league ballgame at Cashman Field," one insider told me. "There was a long line in front of the ticket window. Meanwhile, there was another window marked 'Advance Tickets Only.' No one was in front of this window. So I walked up, put a $20 bill on the counter, and said, 'Give me one ticket for today's game and keep the change.'" He got the ticket.

Be careful, though. A friend of mine took his wife to see a show. He had a $10 bill and a $100 bill. He gave the maître d' the $10 bill to seat them at a nice secluded booth, and later took out his $100 bill to pay for the show. Suddenly he found himself staring at Alexander Hamilton instead of Ben Franklin. He'd given the maître d' the $100 bill by mistake! "No wonder I got such a nice booth," he lamented later.

You can get a good seat one of two ways. Tell the maître d' that you want to sit ringside and that you will take care of the captain. (Then tip the captain who seats you, but only after you're given a seat that you like.) Or if the maître d' studies the seating list for what seems like an eternity, tip him instead. For good service, $10 to $20 is enough. For excellent service, the keys to your car should suffice.

On one occasion, my wife and I joined two other couples for dinner at a new seafood restaurant near the Strip. The place was crowded and they didn't take reservations. "It'll be about an hour," the hostess told us. One of the men in our group whispered something to her, or so I thought. Moments later, we were ushered inside and seated at a circular table right in the middle of the room. The hostess even gave each of us one of her business cards.

"What did you say to her?" I asked my friend in amazement.

"I didn't say anything," he replied. "I gave her $40."

One thing to remember is that even if a hotel is sold out, there is still a block of rooms set aside by the casino for high rollers. The casino also holds back tables in the showroom and hotel restaurants. The maître d' also holds his own tables, which gives you a chance to act like a high roller. Go ahead, be obscene and flash the green.

## Taking Pictures in a Casino

In the old days, taking pictures in a casino was absolutely forbidden. The thinking behind this was that a bank president from some place like Dubuque might be bellied up to a crap table, and there was no telling what would happen if his photograph showed up in his hometown newspaper. It could cause a run on the bank.

Today, however, people will take pictures whether the casinos like it or not. I even see people strolling through the casino with their Camcorders rolling. Actually, most casinos encourage photo opportunities—as long as you're not in a gaming area. You can get your picture taken with Caesar and Cleopatra at Caesars Palace (free). You can get your picture taken in front of $1 million in cash at the Horseshoe (free). You can get your picture taken with the MGM lion (free). But don't take a picture of Uncle Frank playing a slot machine. Photography in the casino gaming area is not allowed. After all, that bank president from Dubuque might still be at the crap table.

## Tipping

To insure promptness. That's what a tip was originally meant for. However, it has become an almost mandatory way of getting the customer to pay the employee's salary while the owner sits in Acapulco counting his profits. Most service-industry personnel make minimum wage or union scale and they rely on tips to earn a living.

Ask any Vegas worker who the best tippers are. Without a moment's hesitation the answer will be high rollers and middle-aged American males. Generally, the worst tippers are Canadians, Europeans, Canadians, young American males, Canadians, and professional people such as doctors and lawyers. On the other hand, South Americans and Asians either tip extremely well or not at all. White American females tip the most while playing blackjack. White American females tip the least at baccarat and craps.

In defense of European gamblers, many don't realize that American tip-earners keep their gratuities. In most European casinos, tips are split equally between the casino and the government. All the tip-earner gets is his salary. Here's something else you may not know. In the majority of American casinos, the dealer's tips are divided equally with the tips of the other dealers. A noted high roller once gave a blackjack dealer a $175,000 tip. She deposited this tip in the dealers' "toke" box. After the money was divided equally, she wound up with only $1,700—which was still enough to cover her yacht payment.

Tipping is a personal matter, and you don't have to follow any set rules. Tipping can mean "Thank you." It can also mean "Please," "I'm sorry," and "Help!" Nothing works better than good old American currency. Before you leave home, convert $20 or $30 into $1 bills. Carry them in your pocket and distribute them freely and you'll get around just fine in Las Vegas.

**Cab drivers.** Fifteen percent of the total fare, but never less than a dollar. Otherwise, he will tell the other four cab drivers in Las Vegas and you'll never get a ride back to the airport.

**Skycaps.** The manual says 50¢ to $1 per bag, depending on size and weight. The problem is trying to figure out how much the skycap weighs.

**Valet parking attendants.** Standard is $1, but double that if the service is extra quick and your car is still in one piece.

**Guest room attendants.** About $1 per day, usually at the end of your stay. Want extra shampoo, plenty of fresh towels, and the keys to the room next door? Then give the attendant the money when you first check in.

**Bartenders.** A dollar a round, or around a dollar.

**Cocktail waitresses.** A dollar a round, or they're bound to holler.

**Keno runners.** A dollar occasionally, whether you lose a little or lose a lot.

**Change personnel.** Technically, you should give the change person from 5% to 10% of your winnings from a jackpot. Of course, on a big jackpot that's hard to do. A simple rule of thumb is to keep counting out coins until the attendant smiles. If you hit a jackpot of $1,000 or more, give the change attendant $50 and give another $20 to the slot person who pays you. If you hit a $1 million jackpot, give the attendant $1,000, give the other players the high sign, give your friends a kiss, give your relatives the gate, and give the boss your notice.

**Bellmen.** $2 to $5 for taking your luggage to your room. Bellmen are a great source of information and advice, and they know something you don't. Namely, where your *&$# room is!

**Showroom servers.** $5 to $10 for a drinks-only show, $10 to $20 for a dinner show depending on how good the food is and if it's still lukewarm by the time it gets to your table.

**Security guards.** $5 to $10 if they save your friend's life; $50,000 if they save *your* life.

**Floor supervisors.** It is against casino policy for floor supervisors to accept money, so don't even bother trying. However, there is nothing in the rule book that says supervisors can't accept gifts. If a supervisor has been helpful, give him a tie, or give her a pretty scarf. Enclose a $50 bill, and gift wrap it.

**Dealers.** This is touchy, because dealers have absolutely no sense of humor. If I word this the wrong way,

I could wind up on *Unsolved Mysteries*. The way it was explained to me by a group of dealers in the soundproof basement of the Horseshoe was, "If you win, give the dealers half your profits. If you lose, give the dealers whatever you've got left." At least, I think that's what they said. It's hard to remember now, because I wasn't able to write it down. I was handcuffed to a chair at the time.

Dealers call tips "tokes." Why they call them tokes is a mystery in itself. Presumably, it's because the word tokes is short for tokens, which is short for gaming tokens, which is short for casino gaming tokens. Dealers also refer to chips as "checks." So don't ask for chips. Ask for checks. Now you won't look like a tourist.

You can either give the dealer a ~~tip~~ toke, or you can bet a ~~chip~~ check for the dealer next to your ~~chip~~ check. When you win, the dealer wins.

Keep in mind that the dealer will never ask you for a tip. This is called hustling, und das is verboten in der casino! In other words, you have to tip without being asked to do it. The way I learned to tip was when I won $278.50 at a $1 blackjack table downtown. As I started to leave, I detected a tear slowly trickling down the dealer's cheek. Later I learned this is known as "soft" hustling. (Dealers are trained to cry.)

But you will be surprised how quickly a dealer will snap to attention when you make a bet for him. He will teach you how to play the game properly and he will steer you away from the casino's battery of bad bets. By all means, tip the dealer. It will be money well spent. Now will you take these handcuffs off, please?

# 10
# Before You
# Leave Home

Las Vegas hotels are booked at 90% capacity most of the time. Therefore it's important to make hotel reservations before you come to Las Vegas. Otherwise, you might wind up staying in some purple motel on the outskirts of town with a sign over your bed reading "George Washington Slept Here." (And probably on the same sheets.)

Remember that every hotel of note in Las Vegas has a toll-free 800 number, so it doesn't cost you anything to make a reservation and it'll save you some anxious moments when you first arrive. You can also set up a casino credit line by phone before you come, and then you won't have to worry about standing at the cashier's cage filling out all kinds of forms.

Call your favorite resorts and ask for free literature. That way, you'll know of upcoming special events, as well as who's playing in the hotel showrooms. Some resorts will even send funbooks that include two-for-one meals and other discounts. Once you're in Las Vegas, you can easily find out who's where by picking up a complimentary issue of *Tour Guide, Today In Las Vegas,* or *What's On*. These magazines can usually be found in the hotel registration area.

If you make a special request with your reservation, you will hear this phrase: "Based on availability." You can request a non-smoking room, you can ask for a room with a nice view, or you can request one that's near the elevators—it's all based on availability. That means these rooms go to the first people who check in each day. If you arrive later in the day, all the non-smoking rooms, or those near the elevators, or those overlooking the pool may be gone. In that case, you're stuck with whatever's left—but you will get a room.

A room reservation is a contract. If the hotel accepts your reservation, it has to give you a room. If the hotel is overbooked, it must find you a room somewhere else. This is called "walking a guest." If this happens to you, make sure you're happy with the other hotel's location before you check in. After all, location is 50% of what you're paying for.

Another phrase you will come across is "double occupancy." If a room is advertised for $25 double occupancy, the price you'll pay is $50. That's because the rate is based on two people sharing the room, with each paying $25. Even if you check in alone, it'll cost you $50. Occasionally, you will even see rooms advertised at a certain price based on *triple* occupancy. Now you're paying three times the advertised price.

Granted, it's misleading. So are those billboards you see when driving into Las Vegas on any major highway: "Rooms $9.99." Then in small letters underneath, "Based on availability." So you pull in and the desk clerk tells you, "I'm sorry, those rooms are all sold out. But we do have a nice room on the 32nd floor for $27."

What if you get to your room and find it doesn't live up to your expectations? It's possible to upgrade your room, sometimes for no additional charge, but once again, this is all based on availability. One hotel manager told me, "It's pretty much impossible to get your room upgraded on a weekend." If it's the middle of the week and the hotel has other rooms available, you will usually be moved with no questions asked. I've heard of couples spending the night in the hotel's honeymoon suite at no extra charge—simply because they had the nerve to complain.

Let's say you check into your room, then something unforeseen happens. The power goes off in the middle of the night and you have to sleep on a chaise lounge out by the swimming pool for four hours. Or the commode overflows, or the air conditioner wakes you up every time it goes on, or the people in the next room decide to have a party at 3 a.m.

Call the front desk and complain. Then complain again when you check out. They will have a record that you complained before, and you might get a partial refund on your room or possibly a discounted rate on your next stay. Here's what happened to a friend of mine in a Las Vegas hotel. At 7 o'clock in the morning, two maids decided to carry on a long-distance conversation, shouting back and forth to each other from opposite ends of the hallway. My friend voiced his displeasure when he checked out, and as a result was only charged for one night of a two-night stay.

No hotel likes to inconvenience a guest, especially in these competitive times. After all, once you've seen the volcano at the Mirage or the theme part at the MGM Grand, what will keep you coming back again and again? It's customer service, the way you're treated at a particular hotel. Many casinos in Las Vegas now have mandatory customer-service and hospitality classes for employees, and a complaint from a guest can cause heads to roll. If you're inconvenienced for any reason, don't hesitate to let somebody know about it.

What if you book a room at a certain price, then get to Las Vegas and find your hotel is offering a discounted room rate? Tell the clerk you want your room at the lower price. A hotel vice president told me that in such cases, you will get the same discount.

If you plan to gamble in Las Vegas, you should learn

as much about it as you can before you get to town. Study the chapters on your favorite games in this book. Learn the odds. Memorize the bets you should make and the ones you should avoid. For a quick refresher course once you get to Las Vegas, turn on the TV in your room and tune in to the gaming instruction channel. Don't gamble your money without doing your homework.

Another way to prepare is to subscribe to the *Las Vegas Advisor* monthly newsletter. Published by gaming expert Anthony Curtis, this nifty periodical gives you a real insider's look that will help you save time and money when you get to town: everything from the Top Ten Values and the best funbook to dates of tournaments and room specials. An annual subscription to the *Las Vegas Advisor* costs $50 a year; and it comes with a great package of discount coupons. Or just order a single issue for the month you're coming for $5. Call 1-800-244-2224. Inside Nevada call 702-252-0655.

Since you're spending your money in the casino, you might want to try to get some of it back by investing in the company. Bally's, IGT, Mirage, Hilton, Circus Circus, Harrah's, Aztar (Tropicana), and ITT (Caesars Palace, Desert Inn) are just a few of the industry's popular stocks on Wall Street, and you might want to look at these companies from an investment standpoint. To learn more about your favorite resort, get an annual report mailed to you free of charge simply by calling the casino. You should also consider subscribing to the *Gaming Industry Weekly Report*. It's the most thorough publication of its kind on gaming stocks. (Call 1-800-990-1902 for a free two-week subscription.)

One of the biggest decisions families have to make before coming to Las Vegas is whether or not to bring the kids. In the old days, it wasn't advisable. After all, there wasn't much for youngsters to do in Vegas. But in recent years, Las Vegas has been transformed into a family-resort destination in an attempt to increase tourism.

The reasoning behind it is if parents can't bring their kids, they won't come either.

During the summer, the kids will gladly spend the whole day at Wet 'n Wild. Or you can park them in a hotel video arcade. Every major casino has one. Don't forget the theme park at the MGM Grand and the circus acts and indoor amusement park at Circus Circus. I also like the Scandia Family Fun Center; it's south of the Palace Station casino on Rancho Drive. Scandia has three elaborate miniature golf courses, an armada of bumper boats, automated baseball pitching machines, and gasoline-powered go carts on the Little Indy Raceway. The park is open year-round.

Most casinos have special rates for children. Cribs are available at just about every hotel in town and front-desk personnel can refer you to babysitting services. Some hotels, though, offer much more. The child-care center at the Gold Coast, for example, offers a free two-hour stay for kids, under the watchful eyes of bonded child-care specialists. (Kids must be potty-trained and over two years of age.)

At Boulder Station and Sunset Station are the New Horizon Kid's Quest child-care facilities for children six weeks to 12 years of age. Activities include a construction lane (building blocks), the Quest (35 different components for climbing, crawling, and sliding), fascination stations (art and puzzle solving), Barbieland (dolls), laser karaoke (singalongs complete with costume chest), a mini-arcade, a movie room, and a tiny tot room specially designed for infants and toddlers. Cost is $5 per hour for each child. Also, the off-Strip Orleans Hotel & Casino has Kid's Tyme, which is similar.

One of the most innovative children's facilities is the MGM Grand Youth Center. Supervised by professionally trained youth counselors, this self-contained facility is for children (ages 3 to 12) of hotel guests and visitors. Open daily from 8 a.m. to midnight, the Youth Center features an arts and crafts room, Super Nintendo, ping-pong, mini-pool tables, hockey and basketball group activities, board games, and a complete preschool room. Daily meals and supervised theme park outings are also available.

In summary, I've told you all the things you should do before you come to Las Vegas. Now I'll tell you one thing you shouldn't do. Don't tell your friends where you are going. They'll ask you to either bring them back a souvenir or make a bet for them. If you tell them they won, they'll be happy, of course. But if you tell them they lost, they won't believe you.

So do yourself a favor. Tell your friends about your trip to Las Vegas—after you get back home.

## Toll Free Reservation Numbers

Alexis Park ................ 1-800-582-2228 ......... (Off the Strip)
Arizona Charlie's ........ 1-800-342-2695 .............. (Suburbs)
Bally's ..................... 1-800-634-3434 ......... (On the Strip)
Barbary Coast ............ 1-888-227-2279 ......... (On the Strip)
Binion's Horseshoe ..... 1-888-237-6537 .......... (Downtown)
Boulder Station .......... 1-800-683-7777 .. (Boulder Highway)
Bourbon Street ........... 1-800-634-6956 ......... (Off the Strip)
Caesars Palace ........... 1-800-634-6661 ......... (On the Strip)
California ................... 1-800-634-6255 .......... (Downtown)
Circus Circus ............. 1-800-634-3450 ......... (On the Strip)
Continental ............... 1-800-634-6641 ......... (Off the Strip)
Debbie Reynolds ........ 1-800-633-1777 ......... (Off the Strip)
Desert Inn ................. 1-800-634-6906 ......... (On the Strip)
El Cortez.................... 1-800-634-6703 .......... (Downtown)
Excalibur .................. 1-800-937-7777 ......... (On the Strip)
Fiesta ....................... 1-800-731-7333 .............. (Suburbs)
Fitzgeralds ................ 1-800-274-5825 .......... (Downtown)
Flamingo Hilton ......... 1-800-732-2111 ......... (On the Strip)
Four Queens .............. 1-800-634-6045 .......... (Downtown)
Fremont..................... 1-800-634-6182 .......... (Downtown)
Gold Coast................. 1-888-402-6278 .............. (Suburbs)
Golden Gate ............. 1-800-426-1906 .......... (Downtown)

Golden Nugget .......... 1-800-634-3454 ........... (Downtown)
Hard Rock Hotel ........ 1-800-HRD-ROCK ...... (Off the Strip)
Harrah's ................... 1-800-634-6765 ......... (On the Strip)
Imperial Palace .......... 1-800-634-6441 ......... (On the Strip)
Lady Luck ................. 1-800-523-9582 ........... (Downtown)
Las Vegas Club ........... 1-800-634-6532 ........... (Downtown)
Las Vegas Hilton ......... 1-800-732-7117 ......... (Off the Strip)
Luxor ....................... 1-800-228-1000 ......... (On the Strip)
MGM Grand .............. 1-800-929-1111 ......... (On the Strip)
Main Street Station ...... 1-800-465-0711 ........... (Downtown)
Maxim ..................... 1-800-634-6987 ......... (Off the Strip)
Mirage ..................... 1-800-627-6667 ......... (On the Strip)
Monte Carlo .............. 1-800-311-8999 ......... (On the Strip)
New Frontier ............. 1-800-634-6966 ......... (On the Strip)
New York-New York .... 1-800-693-6763 ......... (On the Strip)
Orleans .................... 1-800-675-3267 ............... (Suburbs)
Palace Station ............ 1-800-634-3101 ............... (Suburbs)
Jackie Gaughan's Plaza 1-800-634-6575 ........... (Downtown)
Reserve .................... 1-888-899-7770 ............... (Suburbs)
Rio ......................... 1-800-888-1808 ............... (Suburbs)
Riviera .................... 1-800-634-6753 ......... (On the Strip)
Sahara..................... 1-800-634-6666 ......... (On the Strip)
Sam's Town .............. 1-800-634-6371 .. (Boulder Highway)
San Remo ................. 1-800-522-7366 ......... (Off the Strip)
Santa Fe .................. 1-800-872-6823 ............... (Suburbs)
Showboat ................. 1-800-826-2800 .. (Boulder Highway)
Silverton .................. 1-800-588-7711 ............... (Suburbs)
Stardust ................... 1-800-634-6757 ......... (On the Strip)
Stratosphere ............. 1-800-99-TOWER ....... (Off the Strip)
Sunset Station ........... 1-800-786-7389 ............... (Suburbs)
Texas Station ............ 1-800-654-8888 ............... (Suburbs)
Treasure Island .......... 1-800-944-7444 ......... (On the Strip)
Tropicana................. 1-800-634-4000 ......... (On the Strip)
Vacation Village ......... 1-800-658-5000 ............... (Suburbs)

# 11
# Where to Go

You're here! Your plane has landed at McCarran Airport. The first thing you want to do is to go to your room and freshen up. So you hail a taxi. Watch the cab driver carefully. Some of them have been known to take cute little side trips that show you the city up close, but take 15 minutes longer to get to your hotel. The best way to avoid this is by telling the driver exactly where you want to go when you first enter the cab. Say with authority, "I'm going to Luxor (or Caesars or the Tropicana or Circus Circus)." If it's during rush hour or prime time on the Strip, you might also tell him, "Take the freeway—let's avoid traffic." (The freeway is twice as long, but twice as fast.) If it's an odd hour and traffic is light, tell him, "Take Tropicana Avenue to The Strip. There won't be much traffic." Try to give the cab driver the message that

**CASINO SECRET** If you're traveling from the airport to downtown alone or with one other person, take a Gray Line or Bell Trans shuttle. Twenty-four hour service is available for $4.50 one way per person. This compares with about $20 for a cab.

you've been in Las Vegas before and know the way. This is good advice for taking a taxi from the airport to a hotel in any city in the world.

Unless you plan on doing some sightseeing, it's not really necessary to rent a car. For one thing, traffic is pretty tough. Remember, there are more than a million people living in this town and another hundred thousand tourists clogging the streets and freeways. Also, a lot of places are within walking distance of your hotel; city buses and a Strip trolley run frequently; cabs are plentiful; and you can even catch free shuttles around town.

Okay! So here you are in the fastest-growing city in the world, where practically anything goes and usually does. Thirty wedding chapels, 280 churches, millions of meals served a year in 75 major hotels and 700 restaurants, 75% of the work force directly or indirectly employed by the casino industry, enough sequins on showgirl costumes to fill a dozen moving vans, and technicolored megaresorts everywhere you look. Now that you're here, what do you do? Where do you go? What do you see? Read on.

# 12
# The Strip

On a hot summer day in 1937, California hotel owner Tommy Hull was on his way home after spending a few days gambling in downtown Las Vegas. At the intersection of San Francisco Street and Highway 91 (now Sahara Avenue at Las Vegas Boulevard), Hull's car got a flat tire. As he sat waiting for his driver to change it, he began to count the number of cars going by, many of them with out-of-state license plates. Then and there he decided to build a hotel on that spot, paying $5,000 for a 66-acre piece of land, or a little over $75 an acre. From these humble beginnings came Hull's El Rancho Vegas, and the founding of the Las Vegas Strip.

Eighteen months after El Rancho Vegas opened in 1941, the rambling Last Frontier (now the New Frontier) threw open its ranch-style doors. Tourism was going up, and so were land prices. R. E. Griffith paid $1,000 an acre for five acres of land, turning a tiny nightspot called the Club 91 into the Strip's second big resort. The original owner of the Club 91 was Guy McAfee, a former Los Angeles cop-turned-gambler. It seemed that people were always asking McAfee where his club was, and he would tell them, "It's out on the Strip," meaning the road to Los Angeles. This reference was a carryover from McAfee's years in Hollywood, where the original Sunset Strip was located. Others began using McAfee's word for the Vegas highway, and that's how the Strip got its name.

At about this same time, Benjamin "Bugsy" Siegel hit town. He was charged by business associates with building and running a new hotel called the Flamingo. This was nothing new for Bugsy. He was used to being charged with things: assault, burglary, bookmaking, bootlegging, extortion, hijacking, narcotics, white slavery, murder. It wasn't until the 1969 arrival of Howard Hughes, who spent $300 million on casinos and raw land, that the city began to shake off its mob ties. Even then, it took another 15 years for the last vestiges of organized crime to be banished from Las Vegas.

Today, the city is as respectable as Disneyland or any other tourist destination. And the Strip, now the most dazzling and glamorous roadway in the world, is where your trip to Las Vegas really begins.

# Caesars Palace

With luxuriant landscaping, chiseled statuary, and sparkling fountains, Caesars Palace is probably the most recognizable resort in Las Vegas. It looks like a gigantic wedding cake, and the view is better at night when blue lights filter through the hotel's lacy stonework. One-third of Las Vegas visitors tour this modern-day Roman Empire, which will be more splendid by the end of the century. New owners (and they seem to change daily) have recently endeavored to give the property a $900 million facelift.

You're liable to see a movie star or a business czar, and at the very least you will hobnob with royalty. Julius Caesar himself roams these mighty chambers. Dressed regally in flowing robes and Roman armor, he was once stopped by a camera-toting tourist. "Excuse me," the tourist said to Caesar. "Do you work here?"

**See the statue of David in the Appian Way shopping arcade.** Carved from the same marble as Michelangelo's original, this life-sized replica cost $50,000 to build and $100,000 to ship from Turin, Italy. Great photo opportunity.

**See Cleopatra's Barge.** It actually bobs in a pond of water, but watch your head. A hand-carved buxom lass graces the ship's bow, and parts of her can get dangerously close.

**Catch an IMAX spectacle.** Why go to a movie in your hometown when you can fly all the way to Las Vegas to see one? The Omnimax Theatre (in the Olympic Casino) features reclining seats, a panoramic floor-to-ceiling screen, and 10 banks of speakers. Bring your own popcorn. Price: $7 for adults, $5 for kids under 12, seniors over 55, and active military.

Caesars' newest IMAX attraction is the **Race for Atlantis** motion-simulator thrill ride. As part of the experience, each rider is outfitted with an electronic headset that helps produce the ride's unique and immersive environment. Located at the east end of the Forum Shops, this 3-D hydraulic-seat heartstopper is $9.50 for adults and $6.75 for children under 12—and purchasers get a $1 discount good at the Omnimax.

**See the Forum Shops.** Dollar for dollar, this is the most successful shopping center in the world. I went to its grand opening in 1992, and was so inspired by what I saw that I put my thoughts down on paper.

### The Mall of the Roman Empire

Once upon a time, Caesars Palace found itself in a dilemma. The resort owned a valuable piece of land next door to the Mirage, but wasn't sure what to do with it. Should they build more guest rooms on the property or make it into an exotic amusement park? Then Caesars chairman Henry Gluck (since retired) read a survey showing that 85% of all travel plans were made by women. Thus, the idea of a glamorous shopping mall came to be.

The mall is known as the Forum Shops, and it tail-ends off Caesars' Olympic Casino. You would think that for almost $200 million they could have come up with a better name for it, but then again, even Caesars Palace sounded kind of goofy when the hotel was built in 1966. And to show you how much the American dollar has plummeted in the last third of a century, the Forum Shops cost three times as much to build as Caesars itself.

Of course, as I understand it, it isn't costing Caesars anything. In fact, Caesars can't lose. The resort is leasing the property to a private company, and all that foot traffic will undoubtedly wind up inside the casino—which is the name of the game in the first place.

Yet when I visited the Forum Shops shortly before its grand opening (along with 4,000 other employees and hangers-on), I must admit I wasn't too excited. After all, Las Vegas already had three big-time shopping malls, so what was the big deal about another one?

I edged through the towering archway at the north wall of Caesars, almost skidding into a slot machine on the glassy marble floor. Then, suddenly, a hundred different images battled for my attention. Bugs Bunny manned a chariot atop the Warner Brothers Studio Store. Water splashed noisily in the nearby Fountain of the Gods. Booming voices and eerie music came from another fountain. Fragile white clouds overhead whispered across the sky. Was I outdoors? Was I indoors? For a moment I didn't know.

I was walking down a cobblestoned Roman street. It was twilight, dawn, then a picture-perfect autumn afternoon. Later I would learn that the barrel-vaulted ceiling was painstakingly hand painted, giving it the look of a soft Mediterranean sky. The lighting technology cycles through a "day" every few hours.

Restaurants and shops on either side of the street beckoned silently: Planet Hollywood, Spago, Stage Deli, Bernini, Louis Vuitton. A millionaire would be at home in this vast hall, where $3,000 suits, $675 slacks, and $75 neckties made nice stuffing for a Gucci suitcase. An ice cream shop was selling the stuff by the scoop for $1.95, and would later sell $6,000 worth of it in a single day's time. The Sweets Factory was hawking candy at $1.79 for a quarter of a pound, and people were shoveling it into plastic bags as fast as they could. No wonder. After checking out the price on a man's suit, the candy was practically free!

Next to the second fountain was an antique shop, and I wandered inside. By the front door was a genuine 1950s jukebox, its glass bubblers lazily changing from purple to amber to green and churning back memories of Fats Domino and Little Willie John. Price: $7,495, including delivery anywhere in the continental United States.

In the show window was a completely rebuilt Whizzer bicycle, and again I was tromping down memory lane. When I was a kid, a Whizzer was the ultimate mode of transportation. It was actually a motorized kit that you hooked up to your bicycle, and when you got to peddling at a certain speed the motor would kick in. The kit sold for $97.50 in those days, which sounds cheap now, but back then was more money than most adults made in a week. Now you could have a Whizzer for only $5,995, or $6,750 if you opted for the one on a black Phantom frame.

I never had a Whizzer. My childhood possessions amounted to a Columbia bike, a secret decoder ring that glowed in the dark, some comic books (or what we used to call funny books), and a Daisy air rifle with a wooden stock. Today all those things would be worth a small fortune, and here I was still working for a living.

Suddenly I heard booming voices again, and out by the fountain the crowd let out a collective gasp. Four 10-foot statues had come to life, talking and moving like real human beings. Laser lightning lashed across the domed ceiling and music filled the air. I stood there awestruck, seeing constellations in the sky that couldn't be real and yet in that magical instant they were as real as you and me.

Then the show was over. I was swept along with the crowd, and with a brief pang of regret I saw the exit up ahead. My visit to the Forum Shops was over. Caesars had pulled off the impossible. It made a believer out of me.

There are two fountain shows at Caesars: Festival Fountain and Atlantis. Both come to life every hour on the hour, and both are free. Get there 15 minutes early for the best spot.

There are also some great places to eat at Caesars: Terrazzo, Hyakumi, Nero's, Palace Court, Empress Court, Bacchanal. Veddy pricey, however. Dinner for two at the Bacchanal will set you back around $200, including tips to the waiter, wine goddess, back massager, grape peeler, and belly dancer. Best bet for down-to-earth prices is the Cafe Roma coffee shop or La Piazza Food Court.

Before leaving Caesars Palace, spend a quiet moment of reflection at the Brahma Shrine. This is an authentic model of one of Thailand's most popular Buddhist shrines, and is said to ward off bad fortune. If you're planning to gamble...well, a visit to a shrine of good luck couldn't hurt.

# The Mirage

A Vegas casino executive recently said, "To be competitive in Las Vegas, you have to damn near offer one of the seven wonders of the world." Steve Wynn's dazzling Mirage Hotel may not compare with Hoover Dam or the Grand Canyon, but chances are it gets just as many visitors.

Within walking distance of Caesars Palace, the Mirage reminds me of a British colonial plantation set back in time a century or so. Lush tropical landscaping highlights a dramatic entrance, which includes roaring waterfalls and a sleepy lagoon shoring up to a sinister volcano. Nestled in palm trees, the resort can be seen for miles, its stark white exterior banded with stripes of gold mirror. Why, it's almost a—mirage. (Ouch.) Incidentally, Wynn paid big bucks to every other business in Las Vegas that had "Mirage" in its title, just so he could have the name all to himself. The owner of one property on the building site wouldn't sell to Wynn, so there is a small apartment house still tucked away in the midst of the hotel complex.

**See the aquarium in the hotel registration area.** This wall-length 20,000-gallon fish tank is home to sharks, tropical fish, and some icky-looking snails.

**Watch the volcano blow its top.** It erupts every 15

**CASINO SECRET** If the wind is blowing at more than 15 miles per hour, there's no volcano show. In that event, signs will be posted along the sidewalk in front of the volcano, and at the hotel entrances. Another tip: Watch the volcano show from Casino Royale across the street. The view is just as spectacular, and it's not as crowded.

minutes from dusk to midnight, weather permitting. Flames, smoke, noise, pickpockets. (Hang on to your wallet or purse.)

**Check out the royal white tiger habitat.** Here's your chance to get a first-hand look at Siegfried & Roy's rare white tigers. The habitat is designed to duplicate their natural home in the Himalayas (not Siegfried & Roy's, but the tigers), and it's free.

**See the Secret Garden of Siegfried & Roy.** Begin with a guided tour of an underwater habitat where bottle-nose dolphins cavort in a million gallons of man-made ocean. You get to watch through glass windows, and it's almost like being in the water with them. Then edge into the Secret Garden sanctuary and come face to face with the exotic wild animals used in S&R's stage extravaganza: a black panther, Asian elephant, white lion of Timbavati, heterozygous white lion and tiger, striped white tiger, snow leopard, and snow white tiger. Price: $10 for adults, kids under 10 (accompanied by adult) get in free.

Strolling through the Mirage is an adventure in itself. You're lost in a Polynesian village, only instead of bumping into scantily clad island girls, you're bumping into slot machines. Take a break. Head for the Lagoon Saloon (who thinks up these names anyway?) and suck up one of the best piña coladas in the civilized world. While you're sitting there in your high-backed rattan chair, enjoy the view of the rain forest. Velvety tropical gardens abound under a glass-enclosed atrium, while smoky mists swirl around orchids and other tropical foliage. Say, isn't that a dwarf canary palm over there by the waterfall? Nope, it's just my wife's uncle from Texas.

Restaurants at the Mirage include Kokomo's, Mikado, Moongate, and Ristorante Riva. Reservations are required, as well as an 8 by 10 Visa card. If these prices are a little rich for your blood, try the California Pizza

Kitchen. The menu features 28 kinds of gourmet wood-fired pizza, including my favorite—pepperoni and cheese.

# Treasure Island

Feast! Plunder! Valet park! Steve Wynn's peach-colored Treasure Island is an 18th century pirate village—complete with rustic buildings, a sparkling bay, a raging sea battle, even a casino. It's "Pirates of the Caribbean" in 3-D, and a definite must-see for landlubbers and scurvy dogs alike.

Take the monorail from the Mirage next door, or walk if it's a pretty day. Look for Skull Point behind Buccaneer Bay, and see if you can figure out why it has such a grisly name. Stand on the wooden dock and watch the waters gently lap down below. (Motorized wave machines make it happen.) Just beyond the bay is the pirate village, jutting out from the walls of an old mission. Aye, it's here, matey, that the excitement begins.

**See the sea battle between the pirate ship *Hispaniola* and the British frigate HMS *Britannia*.** This mock battle in Buccaneer Bay is the best free show you will ever see. The British fire a warning shot that just misses the pirate ship. Boom, the pirates answer: and there's a hole in the British topsail. Kaboom from the British: smoke from the pirate ship. Boom boom: British. Boom: pirate ship. One ship sinks, one stays afloat. Find out who wins every 90 minutes after 4 p.m.

By the way, when you watch the sea battle you will see pirates and sailors tumbling off their ships into the

**CASINO SECRET**

If you're a high-end slot player, look for telephones at the bank of $1 and $5 machines near the Treasure Island Club booth. Players can use these phones to get change, order drinks, or even call their rooms. What's next? Personal video screens!

water below—and they fall into that water no matter how cold it is. So the next time your job starts getting you down, think about those poor stuntmen at Treasure Island.

Now that the show's over, go inside. Decorated in gold and whitewashed tones, the hotel has the feel of an old Caribbean pirate hideaway. No detail is overlooked, from the balcony fashioned out of an old ship stern to the skeleton of a pirate who fought to his death for a treasure chest. There are even chandeliers decorated with human skulls and bones.

Is all this making you hungry? Then head for the Lookout Cafe, the Plank, the Black Spot Grille, or Buccaneer Bay. Bars and shops include the Smuggler's Cantina, Captain Morgan's, The Crow's Nest, The Doubloon Saloon, Damsels in Dis Dress, The Treasure Chest, and Captain Kids. All they need is a jewelry store called Long John's Silver.

**CASINO SECRET** For a memorable night, make reservations for dinner at the Buccaneer Bay Club. The food is excellent, and you can watch the naval battle right from your crescent-shaped window.

**Experience Cirque du Soleil's** *Mystère.* For the price, this is unquestionably the best show in town. It's an artsy kind of circus without the animals, but it has everything else: acrobats, stilt-walkers, clowns, comedians, actors, musicians, magic, and mystery. My wife liked it so much she started crying, and so did I when I got the bill. Price: $64.90 for adults, half price for half pints. Don't worry about the show ending any time in the near future. Treasure Island spokesmen say *Mystère* will be there forever!

**Play in Mutiny Bay.** Before you hoist the Jolly Roger and sail off for other ports, you may want to check out this huge arcade, in the setting of an ancient Moorish castle. It's the best of its kind in Vegas—with all sorts of games and pinball machines. The only problem is that they let kids in there!

# Bellagio

This is Steve Wynn's newest resort on the Las Vegas Strip, which he says is "the single most extravagant hotel on Earth." Inspired by an Italian village that Wynn once saw near Lake Como, this $1.8 billion megaresort occupies the grounds of the old Dunes Hotel. Where the Dunes Miracle Mile Golf Course was once a famous landmark, now a sparkling 12-acre lake fronts the Strip. The man-made lake comes alive with a $30 million choreographed water ballet of lights, music, and special effects every 30 minutes for 15 hours a day.

"It's a hell of a show," Wynn brags.

And it's true! If anyone knows how to put on a hell of a show, it's Steve Wynn. The secret of Wynn's uncanny success can be found in his own words. At the annual American Gaming Summit in Las Vegas, he said it this way:

"So what is it that people care about, regardless of their ethnic, cultural, social, or economic position, when it comes to leisure, relaxation, vacations, and having fun?

"We go where we can stay at a nice place, eat in interesting and different restaurants, shop in provocative and stylish new places, and see unusual entertainment attractions. That's what we all do—every summer, every winter, and every spring when we go on vacations with each other, our families, and our friends."

Make no mistake, Bellagio is expensive. "We're charging a lot for this hotel," Wynn said. "But it's five-star stuff." In fact, Bellagio's mission statement is to become Las Vegas' first five-star and five-diamond property.

Since Bellagio is strictly a high-roller hangout, Wynn has made it extra special in every way. There are sweeping vistas of the lake, the Italian gardens, the lushly landscaped grounds, the waterfalls, the European fountains and pools. In other words, there ain't a bad room in the house.

Private bungalows are clustered between the lake and the main hotel. Stroll through the gardens at sunset, look out across the lake, and pretend you're in Italy or on the Riviera, or anywhere else your imagination takes you. Meanwhile, a giant amber-splashed observatory high atop the 35-story tower makes you feel as though you're in a fairytale lighthouse. And you are, only it is Bellagio.

Rooms: $150 per night, $250 on Fridays and Saturdays.

Restaurants: Nobu, Le Cirque, Chicago's Charlie Trotter's.

Entertainment: The $70 million Cirque du Soleil.

Access: Via the Strip, or by monorail from Wynn's other properties.

**See the Bellagio collection of priceless art, including original paintings by Van Gogh, Picasso, Renoir, Monet, and Miro.** Wynn paid almost $300 million for his gallery of art, and you can see it for free! While you're at it, take a look at the chandelier in the hotel lobby. Wynn commissioned glass artist Dale Chihuly to create this dazzling masterpiece solely for Bellagio.

**See the massive aquarium in the hotel registration area, and the Fantasy Gardens nearby.** With live foliage, birds, and butterflies, each garden changes with the seasons.

**See your checking account go from $2,000 to zero.** Your best bet is to do like other tourists do. Stay in a cheap hotel, then spend the day at Bellagio.

# MGM Grand

If you plan to visit the MGM Grand, take maps, a compass, a canteen, and a backpack. Lewis and Clark couldn't find their way out of this green-tinged goliath. Built on 114 acres of prime Vegas real estate, the billion-dollar MGM Grand is the biggest hotel in the world.

How big is it? The casino is the size of four football fields. There are 18,000 doors, enough to outfit more than 1,600 three-bedroom homes. The air-conditioning system is large enough to cool a small town. If all the beds were stacked on top of one another, the resulting mess would extend two miles high. It takes an average of 22 miles of sheets each day to freshen the beds in the 5,000-room hotel. And it would take 13 years and eight months for one person to sleep in each room! (Well, sooner or later he's bound to find one he likes.)

Like every other new resort in Vegas, the MGM Grand has its own theme. Here the emphasis is on movies and glamour. When it first opened in 1993, you entered the hotel through the mouth of a gigantic lion's head—which should have told you something right there. With a break-even point of $1 million a day, the MGM lion had to eat a lot of people, or at least their wallets. Frankly, though, the entrance wasn't that impressive, so the MGM brass put their heads together and came up with a great idea. Why not replace the lion's head with the whole lion? So they did, only this one is six stories high, and framed by video screens, water fountains, statues, and palm trees.

**See Studio Walk.** The area around restaurant row is now a Hollywood soundstage, with klieg lights overhead to make it even more realistic. Here you'll find such notable icons as the Brown Derby, Farmer's Market, and the Griffith Park Observatory. For movie memorabilia, check out the "Art of Hollywood" store. By the way, that photograph of Madonna and me in the hot tub is not for sale.

You won't go hungry at the MGM. During the first year the hotel was open, chefs cracked 18,000,000 eggs, brewed 292,000 pounds of coffee, and served nearly 4,400,000 donuts, and that was just for breakfast. Thirty thousand meals a day are served in such eating places as:

• Oz Buffet  (Inexpensive)
• One Liners Food Court  (Inexpensive)
• Stage Deli Express  (Inexpensive)
• Mark Miller's Coyote Cafe and Grille (Medium-priced)
• Wolfgang Puck Cafe  (Medium-priced)
• Studio Cafe  (Medium-priced)
• Rainforest Cafe  (Medium-priced)
• Ricardo's  (Medium-priced)
• Brown Derby (Expensive)
• Gatsby's (Expensive)
• Dragon Court (Expensive)
• Tres Visi & La Scala   (Expensive)
• Emeril's New Orleans Fish House ("Will that be cash, credit card, or U.S. Treasury bond?")

## MGM Grand Adventures Theme Park

It isn't as big as Disneyland, and it isn't as exciting as Disneyland. But for the price, it's a nice diversion from the stuffy confines of a casino. Your ticket is a wristband; just show it to get on any ride.

**Lightning Bolt.** One of the park's original attractions, this roller coaster has been reconfigured so that it's faster and longer with climbs of 35 and 70 feet. Three minutes of thrills highlighted by a splash through the Grand Canyon Rapids. **A+**

**SkyScreamer.** This 25-story colossal swing set is part sky-diving and part hang-gliding. Pull your own ripcord and free-fall 100 feet before swooping into a 70 mile-an-hour arc. Not recommended for anyone in their right mind. **A+**

**Over The Edge.** Your hollowed-out log floats past an old sawmill, then makes a couple of stomach-flipping vertical drops. **A**

**Pirate's Cove.** A half-hour live-action show with real pirates fighting, diving, tumbling, and wondering why they're not over at Treasure Island, getting paid twice as much. **A**

**Magic Screen Theatre.** Indoor cinema featuring live entertainment and movies. **B**

**Grand Canyon Rapids.** Your raft whirls through white water rapids. Along the way you'll see an old western gunfight, some water bombs, and a mine explosion. **B-**

**Parisian Taxis.** A bumper car ride. **C-**

**Pedalin' PaddleBoats.** Wake me up when it's over. **F**

Park hours are seasonal. Ticket prices change constantly, and at last report were $12 for adults, $10 for kids, with $2 off for hotel guests. This doesn't include SkyScreamer—which is $22.50 for one rider, $35 for two, $37 for three. Again, prices are subject to change.

**CASINO SECRET** Take a ride on the MGM Grand Monorail to Bally's. This one-mile dual-lane track links the two most exciting corners in Vegas, and it's free!

# Bally's

What do Bally's and the MGM Grand have in common? The MGM Grand is the largest hotel in the world; Bally's was once the largest. Both were built by Kirk Kerkorian, who is the shortest billionaire in the world.

Kerkorian opened the hotel in 1973 and called it the MGM Grand. Bally Manufacturing bought it in 1986 and changed the name to Bally's. Kerkorian took the money, quadrupled it by buying and selling a couple of other casinos, then built the new MGM Grand. The two properties are connected by a mile-long monorail that eventually may extend all the way to McCarran Airport, and possibly on to Rhode Island.

You enter Bally's via a dramatic grand entry called Bally's Plaza. It isn't much to see in the daytime, but after dark it's absolutely gorgeous. Exotic lighting, wave machines, fountains, music, nice landscaping, and four people movers that silently whisk you inside. Complete show every 20 minutes.

Bally's is one of the few resorts in Vegas with two major showrooms—the Celebrity Room featuring stars like Paul Anka and George Carlin, and the Jubilee Theater where the extravagant production show, *Jubilee*, has been playing since 1981. Interesting facts: 70 sets and backdrops are used in *Jubilee*, more than 4,200 pounds of dry ice are melted for special effects each week, 10 pounds of explosives are detonated nightly, and more than 1,000 costumes are worn during each show. *Jubilee* cost $10 million to produce, but you can see it for $46.

Expensive restaurants: Seasons, Bally's Steakhouse, al Dente, Chang's.

Medium-priced restaurants: Terrace Cafe, Sidewalk Cafe, Big Kitchen Buffet.

Greasy spoons: Sbarros, Stage Deli, Monorail Sushi.

Bally's also has the most opulent buffet in town: the Sterling Brunch. Served Sundays from 9:30 a.m. to 2:30

p.m., it's a cornucopia of imported champagne, caviar, sushi, lobster, rack of lamb, chilled shrimp, shucked oysters, filet mignon, scrumptious pastries, and fresh-squeezed orange juice. Price: $49.95 per person. Reservations suggested.

If you're a high roller, you can become a member of Bally's 22nd Club. This exclusive lounge is on the 22nd floor of Bally's main tower. Designed as a hideaway for high-end players, it offers such amenities as special services check-in, preferred valet parking, VIP reservations, free continental breakfasts, free cocktails and hors d'oeuvres, and a spectacular view of the city.

If you are not a high roller…well, you can still get a nice view of the city by taking the stairs up to the 26th floor.

# Las Vegas Hilton

What do Bally's, the MGM Grand, and the Las Vegas Hilton have in common? At one time, each was the largest hotel in the world; they were all built by zillionaire Kirk Kerkorian. The dramatic entry is highlighted by solid glass walls, brass-handled doors, cobblestone paving, polished marble floors, crystal chandeliers, and silk flower arrangements.

Originally named the International, it's the only megaresort in town that doesn't front the Las Vegas Strip. It's on Paradise Road next to the Convention Center, which is the main reason why it's such a successful operation. That, and the fact that Elvis Presley made his comeback there in the early 1970s. Presley fans still flock to the resort, hoping to catch one more glimpse of their favorite star.

"There he is!"

"No, that's just our busboy."

"There he is!"

"No, that's my wife's uncle from Texas."

"There he is!"

"No, that's the Goodyear blimp."

**See the Elvis Collection.** Included is a jumpsuit worn by Elvis, his guitar, and a bronze-cast statue of the King. It's in the main lobby and it's free.

**See "Star Trek: The Experience."** Paramount and the Las Vegas Hilton have joined forces to bring Star Trek to life. This dazzling interactive adventure consists of 10 actors, five different environments, and two motion simulators. Pass through the futuristic Space Quest casino and into the Star Trek museum. At the far side of the museum is The Experience. Here you'll beam aboard the bridge of the U.S.S. *Enterprise,* then blast through distant galaxies at warp speed. After you shoot down a few dastardly Klingons, it's on to Quark's Bar where you can rehash your adventures. Price: $9.95 for Nevada residents, $14.95 for everyone else.

**Make a bet at the Las Vegas Hilton Race and Sports Superbook.** Voted the best sports book in Las Vegas year after year, this state-of-the-art sports facility boasts the largest public video wall in the world, second in size only to (non-public) NASA. With 40 video screens fed by 14 satellite dishes, you can watch nearly every major sporting event or race being televised at any given time. The Hilton Superbook is a popular spot for football bettors, since the Hilton issues the country's first nationally recognized betting line each week for both pro and college football.

The Super Contest, one of the top handicapping contests in the country, takes place at the Superbook each week during professional football season. Pay a $1,500 entry fee, pick five pro games against the Superbook line, and win as much as $150,000. Just remember, though, that you're competing against some of the nation's best handicappers.

> **CASINO SECRET**
>
> Take advantage of the Hilton Superbook "Nickel Line" on Thursdays, and wager only -105 ($10.50 to win $10) on college and professional football bets. It's -110 almost everywhere else. This drops the casino's advantage from 4.5% to 2.4%.

The Las Vegas Hilton has some great restaurants, including Bistro Le Montrachet, Andiamo, Hilton Steakhouse, Barronshire, Garden of the Dragon, MargaritaGrille, and one of my favorites—Benihana Village. This enchanting Japanese fantasyland sends you off to the Orient, where you will see thunder and lightning storms, lush Japanese gardens, gurgling streams, winding foot paths, and an authentic Torii Arch soaring high above you. Have cocktails and hors d'oeuvres at Benihana's Kabuki Lounge, then eat at the Benihana Seafood Grille (nice aquarium at the entrance), or at Hibachi, where a chef chops, dices, and stir fries right at your table. Suggestion: Bring another couple. If it's just you and your wife or husband, you're liable to find yourself seated with a couple of complete strangers.

Golfers will love the Las Vegas Hilton Country Club. The par-71 course, with five lakes and plenty of trees, is only 10 minutes away. Hotel guests receive special rates and preferred tee times. Get a hole in one on the par-five 14th hole and receive a free golf ball with the Hilton logo on it. Mine is displayed over my fireplace.

# Flamingo Hilton

This is where it all started over 50 years ago. In 1945, the Las Vegas Strip was a strip, all right. It was a strip of sand and cactus almost ten miles from downtown. Then Benjamin "Bugsy" Siegel—gambler, murderer, entrepreneur—came up with a great idea. Why not build a casino out there? The land was dirt cheap, and it was right on the old L.A. Highway coming in from California. Bugsy made some phone calls and the next thing you know he had $1 million in his pocket, a couple of silent partners named Meyer Lansky and Lucky Luciano, and a new casino under construction, which he called the Fabulous Flamingo.

The hotel opened a year later. Everyone who worked there, including the janitors, wore tuxedos. Sterling silver place settings graced every table. There were 105 guest rooms, a casino, nine gift shops, a health club, steam rooms, a 40-horse stable, a swimming pool, tennis courts, a nine-hole golf course, and a trapshooting range. Unfortunately, this ran the cost of the Flamingo $5 million over budget. The result was that Bugsy got air-conditioned while reading a newspaper at his girlfriend's house. Meanwhile, the Flamingo went on to become one of Vegas' great success stories.

The Hilton Corporation took the Flamingo under its wing in 1970 and immediately began to make it one of the largest hotel complexes in the world. They did it by adding a tower in 1976, adding a tower in 1980, adding a tower in 1983, adding a tower in 1986, adding a tower in 1990, and adding a tower in 1994. Gosh, I wonder what their next expansion project will be?

Quite frankly, the Flamingo of today is so huge and cluttered that it's almost impossible to get around the place. Its biggest claim to fame is being the roots of the Las Vegas Strip, but these roots have been bulldozed in the name of progress. Alas, Bugsy Siegel's private apartment—with bullet-proof windows and five different exits—is gone.

Restaurants at the Flamingo Hilton include Alta Villa (Italian), Beef Baron (American), Flamingo Room (Continental), Hamada of Japan (Japanese), Peking Market (Chinese), Bugsy's Deli, and Lindy's Coffee Shop.

**Stroll through the wildlife habitat.** This 15-acre water paradise, surrounded by waterfalls and palm trees, is located in the back of the Flamingo. Designed to resemble a secluded island in the Caribbean, the habitat teems with wildlife, including penguins, flamingos, ducks, swans, macaws, cockatoos, turtles, and goldfish.

For a special treat, have lunch at the Paradise Garden Buffet. Glass walls offer a panoramic view of the habitat past a roaring 22-foot waterfall. That alone is worth the price of the meal.

If you stay at the Flamingo, ask for a room in the front tower. It's right across the street from three of the snazziest casinos in town. Watch the fountains at Caesars Palace, the volcano at the Mirage, and the construction of Bellagio, all from the comfort of your own room.

**CASINO SECRET** You can still return to Ground Zero in Las Vegas. The Flamingo finally paid tribute to one of the city's founding fathers with a commemorative plaque honoring Bugsy Siegel. It can be found between the main casino and the pool area. You're standing at the very spot where Siegel's original Flamingo Hotel once stood. Great photo op.

# New York-New York

Yo! Wanna go to New Yawk? It's in Vegas now. The eerie skyline of the Big Apple is off scale by a hair, but from a distance New York-New York looks like the real thing. About the only thing it doesn't have are the muggers!

Across the street from the MGM Grand, 16 famous landmarks rise out of the desert like huge dusty crayons: the New York Public Library, Lever House, the Soldiers and Sailors Monument, 55 Water Street, the Statue of Liberty, Ellis Island, the Empire State Building, the Century Building, Liberty Plaza, the New Yorker Hotel, Grand Central Station, the Seagram Building, the Chrysler Building, the Whitney Museum, the CBS Building, and the Brooklyn Bridge. And twisting around the whole skyline is a genuine Coney Island roller coaster.

It's not just the outside that has the look and feel of New York, but the inside as well, with scene sets from Big Apple neighborhoods everywhere you look. In fact, the carpet in the casino resembles a Gotham street, complete with curbs and crosswalks that guide visitors to different hotel areas. It's a great idea, and one the other megaresorts could use.

Wanna shop? Go to Park Avenue. Wanna find out what's new? Go to Times Square. Wanna set up credit or cash a check? Go to Wall Street. Wanna gamble? Go to Central Park. Wanna eat? Go to Little Italy.

This resort appeals to everyone, because people who have never been to New York want to see what it looks like, and people who have been to New York want to see if it looks like the real thing. Personally, I like New York-New York for another reason. It won't cost you an arm and a leg to stay there. Standard rooms are $89 midweek, and $129 on weekends. And it's right on the Las Vegas Strip, within walking distance of almost every major resort in town.

The Big Apple has the best food in the world, and the Little Apple is doing its best to compete. Try Il Fornaio, an authentic Italian restaurant and bakery with a different menu each month; Chin Chin's, a Chinese dining room that features Polynesian, Pacific Rim, Szechwan, and Cantonese; Gallagher's Steak House for grilled steaks and seafood; and Motown Cafe, a trendy theme restaurant with Motown music, memorabilia, and munchies. The most authentic big-city attraction, though, is the Village Eateries food court, a stunning simulation of the back streets of Greenwich Village, where you'll find hamburgers, New York-style pizza, a Japanese noodle place, Mexican sit-down, and a deli. Upstairs, there's a Nathan's hot dog stand, of course.

Got a death wish? **Ride the "Manhattan Express."** Experience the force of negative gravity on this roller coaster that climbs, banks, loops, spirals, twists, and dives—at speeds up to nearly 70 miles per hour! The ride lasts about four minutes, which is about three and a half minutes too long for the likes of me. Then again, I get dizzy when I lick an airmail stamp. Price: $5, and waits can be as long as 30 minutes.

**See the Coney Island Entertainment Center.** It's like going back to the early 1900s, but with the high-tech gadgetry of today: bumper cars painted to look like New York taxis, shooting galleries, laser tag, midway-style carnival games, even a Daytona-style interactive driving simulator. There's also a free fiber-optic fireworks show overhead and live street entertainment.

Caution. It's estimated that five-million people will crowd into this novel resort each year, which breaks down to about 14,000 people a day. So be prepared to fight the crowds just like you would in real New York. In fact, when I was there I overheard a girl telling her mother, "Let's get the hell outta here!" And the girl was four years old!

That's New York-New York.

# Monte Carlo

Monte Carlo is the first joint-venture casino in Las Vegas. The land is owned by Steve Wynn and the casino is operated by Circus Circus. Styled along the lines of Monaco's opulent Place du Casino, the Monte Carlo brings a taste of Europe to Las Vegas. Fanciful arches, chandeliered domes, marble floors, ornate fountains, and gas-lit promenades highlight the hotel; there's even a Gothic glass registration area overlooking the pool. In these ways, the Monte Carlo of Monaco and its Vegas namesake are much the same.

That, however, is where the similarity ends. In Vegas, you can stroll right into the Monte Carlo wearing a T-shirt and a pair of cutoffs. Try doing that in Monaco and you'll get a nice view of Prince Ranier's moustache as you bounce down the sidewalk. In Monaco, you practically have to be a jet setter or movie star to gain admission to the casino. In Vegas, the Monte Carlo is geared for the mass-market player and everyday tourist. Rooms start at $59, or $129 for suites.

Restaurants include the Market City Caffe for Italian food, the Dragon Noodle Company for Far Eastern dishes, Blackstone's Steakhouse, and the Golden Bagel deli. There's also a unique micro-brewery and bar called the Monte Carlo Brewery Pub, which brews and sells its own beer right on the premises.

While you're there, check out the lavish pool area. There's an "easy river" water ride, some majestic waterfalls, and even a wave pool that will out-splash anything in the dreary old Mediterranean. Or if you'd rather shop, there's a realistic town square accented with old-fashioned facades and lots of stores.

Worth seeing is the ornate Lance Burton Theater, a European-style opera house with elegant turn-of-the-century architecture and a spectacular lobby. It's here that illusionist Lance Burton performs nightly. Twice named

"Magician of the Year" by the Academy of Magical Arts, he was described by Johnny Carson as the best illusionist he's ever seen. For the price ($34.95 a person), it's a great show.

But the best thing about the Monte Carlo is that first breathtaking view from outside. It makes you wonder how Las Vegas ever got along without it.

# Desert Inn

This one's a real sleeper. Everyone who comes to Las Vegas heads for one of the city's theme resorts, and they drive past such famous landmarks as the New Frontier, Sahara, Riviera, and Desert Inn. But spend a couple of leisurely hours at the Desert Inn. You'll have the place practically to yourself.

It was originally called Wilbur Clark's Desert Inn. Construction started in 1946, but Clark (a former California bellhop) ran out of money and wasn't able to finish building it until 1950. He got the extra cash by borrowing it from the Cleveland mob, and by the time they got through with him Clark was left with only 6% ownership in his own hotel. At least, they let him keep his name on the marquee. "The Cleveland Mob's Desert Inn" didn't have quite the same ring to it.

There's history here, folks. This is the hotel where billionaire Howard Hughes took up residency in 1966. Asked to vacate his digs to make way for New Year's high rollers, Hughes bought the joint instead. Twenty years later, it was purchased by gazillionaire Kirk Kerkorian. The ITT Corporation took it over in 1993, spending $200 million on a complete renovation.

The grand lobby of the 150-acre resort has been designed to reflect the long-lost style of the 1930s' Palm Beach era. Large glass windows look out on breathtaking views of one of the most beautiful pool and garden areas you'll ever see. Ducks, peacocks, and exotic birds complement the idyllic setting. This makes a splendid backdrop for the mezzanine Monte Carlo Room, where specialties include duck, peacock, and exotic birds. Just kidding. Seriously, the Monte Carlo Room exudes a certain mystique, and chances are good that if the person seated at the next table looks like a movie star, she probably is. Other eateries at the Desert Inn include Portofino,

HoWan, and the Terrace Pointe coffee shop (same view, cheaper meals).

Want to walk the same fairways as John Kennedy and Lyndon Johnson, or trip over the same sand traps as Gerald Ford? Then play the world-famous Desert Inn Golf Course, the only golf course on the Strip. It's expensive ($195 for non-guests, anywhere from $115 to $145 for D.I. guests), but it's rich in history. In fact, back in 1953 the Desert Inn made headlines when the winner of the course's Tournament of Champions was paid $10,000 prize money in genuine silver dollars.

# Tropicana

When the Tropicana Hotel opened in 1957, it was hailed as "the Tiffany of the Strip." In 1986, it became "The Island of Las Vegas." I've always liked this resort, even back in the late 1970s when it had a giant paint-peeled fountain in front of it. Workmen were constantly emptying it, or filling it, or sanding it, or repainting it, but no matter what they did it always looked the same.

There used to be a cocktail lounge at the Trop called the "Blue Room," and for the price of a drink, you could see some of the country's top entertainers. Many nights I sat there enthralled by the live performances of Louis Armstrong, Sarah Vaughan, Si Zentner, Julie London, or Count Basie. Spending all those evenings in the Blue Room is probably the main reason I never got around to leaving town. The Blue Room is long gone, but the Tropicana has several attractions worth seeing.

**See the Wildlife Walk.** The Wildlife Walk is a bird and wildlife habitat located inside the covered walkway between the Trop's two towers. Here you'll be introduced to some lovable creatures, including cockatoos, African parrots, a crocodile monitor, a Burmese python, a boa constrictor, and some pygmy marmosets. These are among the world's smallest monkeys, one of whom has an uncanny resemblance to a pit boss I used to know. From the walkway, look down on the five-acre Tropicana garden and pool. Lagoons, spas, waterfalls, and the world's largest indoor-outdoor swimming pool will make you wish that clocks had never been invented.

The Tropicana also has the world's only "swim-up" blackjack table. To get to the game, you have to swim up in your bathing suit. You play while sitting in the water. If you've got some soggy paper money with you, no problem. There are rotating drop boxes at the game that can dry the cash in less than a minute. Smile sweetly and the dealer might let you dry your hair in one of them.

**See the *Folies Bergere*.** This is the longest-running production show in Las Vegas. Playing since 1959, it's world-famous for its statuesque topless showgirls and elaborate costumes. Two shows nightly: a dinner show priced from $30.95, and a cocktail show from $23.95.

If you don't want to spend that much, take a backstage tour in the afternoon for $2. Of course, your wife will never speak to you again, but think of the money you'll save. Incidentally, those backstage tours are hosted by former *Folies* showgirls. They'll tell you what it's like to do two shows a night, six nights a week, and still smile while dancing.

Restaurants at the Tropicana include Savannah Steak House; Pietro's for Italian and gourmet fare; Mizuno's teppan dining where chefs prepare the food at your table with razor-sharp precision; Calypso's, a 24-hour coffee shop; Golden Dynasty for Chinese; the Tropics buffet; and the Delicatessen.

The Tropicana is accented with stained glass and brasswork, and plenty of razzle-dazzle improvements that include a $1.4 million baccarat room, new carpeting, a premium slot area, and a facade that gives the place a Victorian South Seas' look. But the main reason for its continued popularity is not appearance so much as location. It's situated smack dab on the top corner in town, with a pedestrian skywalk system that links it with the MGM Grand, Excalibur, and New York-New York.

At the Tropicana you've really got the best of two worlds: the intimacy of the old Las Vegas and the excitement of the new Las Vegas. Worth seeing.

# Imperial Palace

Next door to the Flamingo Hilton, the Imperial Palace looks like a cross between a Vegas casino and a Vietnamese prisoner of war camp. It's a popular tourist hangout, however, because it's cheap ($73 for two nights), and it's in one of the best locations on the Strip.

Built on the site of the old Flamingo Capri Motel, the Imperial Palace is owned by former building contractor Ralph Engelstad, and is one of the few resorts in Las Vegas that hasn't been gobbled up by corporations. It doesn't look that big from the outside, but once you go through the pagoda-like entrance, it seems to stretch for miles.

Hungry? Ask someone wearing a name tag where the heck the restaurants are. These include Ming Terrace, the Embers, the Rib House, Pizza Palace, and the Teahouse. The best of the bunch is the Seahouse, featuring cioppino as good as any in San Francisco. Casual dress, but reservations are suggested.

**Tour the Antique and Classic Auto Museum.** Two hundred antique, classic and special-interest automobiles (from a revolving collection of 750) are on display in what is considered one of the finest collections of its kind in the world.

Among them are James Cagney's Duesenberg, John Kennedy's Lincoln Continental bubbletop, Woodrow Wilson's 1917 Pierce Arrow, Hitler's 1936 Mercedes Benz, Elvis Presley's 1976 Cadillac Eldorado, Howard Hughes' 1954 Chrysler, Tom Mix's 1937 Cord, Marilyn Monroe's 1955 Lincoln Capri, and everyone's favorite: Al Capone's 1930 bullet-proof 1930 V-16 Cadillac. There is also a smattering of military vehicles, motorcycles, trucks, tractors, taxis, fire engines, and even some old-fashioned gas pumps.

Take the elevator at the back of the casino to the 5th floor of the parking garage. Price: $6.95 for adults, $3 for senior citizens and children under 12.

**See *Legends In Concert.*** This long-running revolving-star production has been named "Show of the Year," "Entertainers of the Year," and "Show of Shows." Here's your chance to see Elvis Presley, Marilyn Monroe, Liberace, Buddy Holly, Bobby Darin, Sammy Davis Jr., John Wayne, and Nat King Cole one more time. Lasers and a special projection system create dazzling effects that add to the show's appeal, and some of these lookalikes are just amazing. Price: $29.50 for adults, half-price for children under 12.

**CASINO SECRET**

Want to get into the Classic Auto Museum without paying? There are usually hawkers outside the front entrance who pass out free tickets. Sometimes the brochure racks inside the hotel are filled with free tickets. I got mine from a bartender. The Imperial Palace gives away *two million tickets* a year to the museum. You might as well get yours free, too!

# Circus Circus

The second-oldest theme resort in Las Vegas, Circus Circus opened to rave reviews in 1968. The hotel was the brainchild of Vegas innovator Jay Sarno, who also designed Caesars Palace two years earlier. I was one of those who packed the place the night it opened, and you would understand everyone's excitement if you lived here at the time. Back in the late '60s, a Las Vegas resort was nothing more than a casino with a string of bungalows around it. It was hard to tell which hotel you were in—unless you went outside and looked up at the marquee.

Caesars and Circus Circus changed all that, and Jay Sarno was the man who made it happen. Imagine driving up to a 90-foot high circus tent, a 13-story neon clown rising above you, twinkling street lamps on each corner that resembled clusters of colored balloons, and a permanent circus covering an area of 120,000 square feet. I remember being swept along with the crowd, calliope music warbling in the background and the smell of cotton candy in the air.

There was a booth on the second floor where, for a dollar a ball, you tried to hit a bull's eye 25 feet away. Hit that target, and a bed inside the glass booth tilted sideways. Out of the bed emerged a gorgeous girl, who danced topless for maybe two seconds. (It might have been longer, but it seemed like two seconds.) The attraction was taken out after about two weeks, as I recall. For one thing, Circus Circus was extolling itself as the first family resort in town, and here were those topless girls inside doing the hoochi coochi!

Still, Circus Circus was different. It brought the fun of a real circus to town, with trapeze acts and an exciting midway where you could win kewpie dolls and stuffed animals for your sweetie. And where else could you lose $500 at the crap table, said comedian Shecky Greene, then turn around and step in elephant shit?

The only problem is that Circus Circus never changed. Except for a couple of towers and a sky shuttle, the resort is the same as it was 30 years ago. It's still the flagship of the Circus Circus empire (which includes Excalibur, Luxor, Gold Strike Resorts, and part owner-ship of the Monte Carlo—and that's just in Las Vegas). But it isn't showmanship that brings the people here. It's cheap meals and cheap rooms.

Rooms go for $29 Sunday through Thursday, or a king-sized suite is available for another $20. Prices are higher on weekends, when rooms are $49 and suites are $99.

Circus Circus has the cheapest buffet in town. Twelve thousand people a day line up for the Circus Buffet Spectacular, with over 50 items for each meal. Breakfast is $2.99, lunch $3.99, and dinner $4.99.

Circus Circus also has the best steakhouse in town. Called The Steakhouse, it offers "exquisite dining in a warm atmosphere of casual elegance." I didn't make that up; Circus Circus did. But in this case it's true. Steaks are mesquite-grilled to perfection and the beef is aged right on the premises. Expensive, but worth it.

For the kids, there are free circus acts daily. See acrobats, magicians, jugglers, tightrope walkers, and those daring young men on the flying trapeze. Acts appear daily under the big top from 11 a.m. to midnight.

**CASINO SECRET**

Circus Circus is one of the best places in town to play blackjack. In addition to good rules, the Ringmaster Slot Club is the only one in Vegas to give cash back for table-game play (like the other clubs do for slot play). Just show 'em your card before you play, and later you can pick up a cash rebate from the club booth.

**Visit Grand Slam Canyon.** Directly behind Circus Circus is the pink glass dome of a five-acre indoor amusement park. Climate-controlled for year-round comfort, the park is set in a desert canyon of cliffs, pinnacles, and caverns.

**Canyon Blaster.** The only indoor double-loop, double-corkscrew roller coaster in the country. It's also the only good ride in the place. **A**

**Rim Runner.** Plummet down a wild water trail and get soaking wet in the process. **B**

**Hot Shots.** Hide and seek with laser guns. **D**

**Sand Pirates.** A swinging pirate ship that gives you one good swoop before you're outside standing in line again. **C**

**Canyon Cars.** Bumper cars. **C**

**Mystic Magic Theatre.** Entertainment for all and for all a good night. **C**

There are eight life-sized dinosaurs in the park, a 68-foot waterfall, some Native American cliff dwellings, and a Mexican restaurant called Comida Rica. An all-day pass is $13.95, or $9.95 for kids under 10. Business has been so bad, though, that sometimes they don't even charge. Go when it's free. Otherwise forget it.

# Excalibur

Excalibur, caddy-corner from the MGM Grand, is another Circus Circus property, only here the emphasis is on King Arthur. You see, many centuries ago in the land of Britain, Excalibur was a magical sword embedded in a huge block of stone. The person who could pull that sword from the stone would be crowned King of England. Great knights of highest renown (Bobby Knight, Ted Knight, Gladys Knight) came to free the sword, but alas, all failed. Then came Arthur, a mere squire, who took hold of Excalibur and brought it forth from the stone. Thus began the era of Camelot and another theme for yet another Las Vegas resort.

Excalibur was designed in April 1990, built in May 1990, and opened in June 1990. Oh, wait a minute. I'm getting the high sign from my research staff. I'm sorry, I read the figures wrong. The Excalibur was designed on Monday, June 5; built on Tuesday, June 6; and opened Wednesday, June 7.

Surrounding a Tinkertoy castle, the Excalibur is a $290 million trip to the Middle Ages. It's like Disney's Fantasyland, only here you get to drink and gamble. It's big and it's crowded, so look for overhead signs that can help you find what you're looking for.

**Cheer at *King Arthur's Tournament.*** A royal feast where knights in armor fight to the death, swordplay and chivalry come alive, maidens dance, and Merlin casts his magic spells—and you get to eat with your fingers! Kids love this show. Two performances "knightly." Price: $29.95 and you can reserve tickets up to six days in advance.

**See the Royal Lipizzaner Stallions.** These world-famous animals horse around in King Arthur's Arena. Interesting afternoon diversion for under $10

**Take in the Glockenspiel Fairy Tale.** This free show takes place atop the rotunda towers outside the Excalibur. Stand there and watch; it only lasts about four minutes. It's a whimsical little fairy tale about a beautiful princess who meets a fire-breathing dragon in the woods. Don't despair, it has a happy ending. Just so you can impress your kids, the glockenspiel is powered by 20 motors plugged into a computer program, which is what makes the figures move. And if they ask you what a glockenspiel is, simply say, "C'mon, let's go!"

**Play in the Medieval Village.** Wander past shops and restaurants, while magicians, jugglers, and singers entertain you, and catch the free stage shows every half hour at the Court Jester's Stage. You may also want to check out the Fantasy Faire arcade on the lower level of the hotel: there's a carnival midway inside, as well as two exciting motion simulator rides.

Restaurants at the Excalibur include Camelot, for gourmet dining; Sir Galahad's, a prime rib house in royal surroundings; Wild Bill's Steakhouse, live music and dancing, too; and Sherwood Forest Cafe, a fancy way of saying "coffee shop." Don't worry, they're all good, and the last three are inexpensive.

# Luxor

Luxor's dazzling bronze pyramid, made of 26,783 glass plates, is probably the most unusual structure in a city noted for its novel architecture. Located on the south end of the Strip, it rises regally from the desert floor with a 10-story replica of the Sphinx overlooking the main entrance. It's beautiful, especially at night when Luxor's "Beam of Light" radiates the Las Vegas sky and strobes sprint up and down the four corners of the building.

Luxor opened in 1993. Back then, you felt excitement as you journeyed inside for the first time. For an instant you were Howard Carter, about to break the seal on the tomb of Tutankhamen. Then you found yourself not in the Valley of the Kings, not in some burial chamber filled with gold and other treasures, but inside a giant hangar with no idea where to go.

So Luxor spent almost a quarter of a billion dollars giving the pyramid a complete makeover. Now visitors are greeted by a life-sized replica of the great Temple of Ramses, rising 35 feet from the marbled floors of the world's largest atrium. Luxor also added a 1,200-seat showroom featuring the theatrical odyssey *Imagine*, the Oasis Spa, the Ra nightclub, the Giza Galleria shopping arcade (with talking camels in front), a people mover connecting the Luxor with the Excalibur, and most important: two stepped towers that give the Luxor a grand total of 4,407 rooms—making it the third largest hotel in the world.

Luxor boasts one of the best gift shops in town. The Scarab Shop features a unique collection of Egyptian gifts, souvenirs, and apparel. It also has one of the most unusual gift items anywhere: a personalized T-shirt or sweatshirt with your name spelled in hieroglyphics. On a grander scale, the Source Shop is an elegant gallery that offers genuine Egyptian antiquities. You'll also find reproductions of ancient Egyptian artifacts, including jewelry, paintings, and pottery.

**Explore King Tut's Tomb.** Luxor's biggest attraction is the King Tut Museum, as it was when discovered in 1922. Each meticulously duplicated item found in the tomb is positioned exactly according to records maintained by the Howard Carter expedition. On the way to King Tut's fabulous treasury you'll explore the vestibule, passage, antechamber, annex, and burial chamber of the tomb. This is probably the top educational exhibit in Vegas and definitely worth seeing. The $4 tour takes about 30 minutes. Museum hours are from 9 a.m. to 11 p.m. daily.

**Explore Luxor's Attractions Level.** "In Search of the Obelisk" consists of two motion-simulator rides where you descend to a hidden temple deep below Las Vegas and take a wild tour through the excavations. The IMAX Theater features a 7-story screen, 30,000 watts of sound, and movies in 3-D. "Sega VirtuaLand" is an arcade featuring virtual-reality simulators. You're in the cockpit of a fighter jet, now you're on the speedway dodging other race cars, and the nice thing is you don't have to wear a helmet.

Restaurants at the Luxor include the Sacred Sea Room (seafood), Millennium (cafe), Papyrus (Polynesian), the Pyramid coffee shop, Luxor Steakhouse, the Pharaoh's Pheast Buffet, and a gourmet restaurant called Isis. Named one of the top ten gourmet rooms in the U.S. by Restaurant Guide, Isis offers Continental cuisine in an atmosphere of ancient Egypt. Perfect place for Mummy's Day.

# Stardust

At high noon on July 2, 1958, the Stardust opened on the Las Vegas Strip. It was hailed as the largest resort complex in the world, with $6 rooms and a neon sign so bright it could be seen from three miles away. But it was almost as though the place had a curse on it. Builder Tony Cornero suffered a fatal heart attack before the Stardust even opened. Then it got mobbed—first by the Detroit mob, then the Kansas City mob, then the Chicago mob.

This is the hotel where those infamous characters in the movie *Casino* carved up the pie. In real life, they were Tony "The Ant" Spilotro, Frank "Lefty" Rosenthal, Teamsters lawyer Allan Dorfman, and longtime Vegas boss Carl Thomas. Rosenthal retired to Florida, but the others didn't fare so well. Spilotro and his brother were beaten to death in an Indiana cornfield, Dorfman was shot while walking through a Chicago parking lot, and Thomas died in a mysterious jeep accident.

Those days have thankfully faded into history, and now the Stardust is under the leadership of the highly respected Boyd Gaming Corporation. It doesn't have a theme park or any other state-of-the-art attraction, and frankly it doesn't fit the modern Las Vegas image. But there are plenty of good restaurants and nice bars inside the Stardust, along with one of the largest casinos in town.

William B's Steakhouse features gourmet dining in turn-of-the-century decor. Tres Lobos serves traditional Mexican fare in an open courtyard. Tony Roma's is known for great barbecued ribs and chicken. Toucan Harry's is a 24-hour coffee shop with a Banana Republic theme. Finally, Ralph's Diner features blue-plate specials from $3.95 and an old-fashioned fountain with milk shakes, banana splits, and sundaes. It's like returning to the '50s when Eisenhower was president, cars were cars, and I was in high school chomping at the bit to get out of high school. Oh well, we can't go back, but Ralph's Diner is the next best thing. And you might just see Ralph's waitresses slippin' and slidin' to the music of those glorious times—especially if you throw your greasy napkin on the floor. Recommended.

**CASINO SECRET**

For a real blast from the past, you can park your car where Lefty Rosenthal's Cadillac got blown up. In real life it happened in the parking lot of Tony Roma's barbecue joint on East Sahara. In the movie *Casino*, it was filmed in the parking lot of Main Street Station downtown.

# Riviera

The Riviera was the first high-rise hotel in Las Vegas, towering nine stories above the Strip when it opened in 1955. It was also the first resort in Las Vegas to bring superstars to town and pay them super prices.

Liberace made his debut in the Riviera showroom at an unheard-of salary of $50,000 a week. Later he remembered opening night. "It was one of the great nights of my career. When the curtain went up, the ovation was tremendous. So was my bank account from that day forward."

Locals call it "the Riv," and today the emphasis is more on gambling than on family-style entertainment. At one time, the Riviera had plans to build a huge Ferris wheel inside the hotel, a hook to lure families from other resorts. The idea was scratched, though, and the Riv's new motto is, "We're the entertainment center of Las Vegas, and the alternative for grown-ups."

The flashy-colored facade of the Riviera is a far cry from its distinctive lines of days gone by, but it still has great atmosphere and great food.

Ristorante Italiano features the earthy cooking of northern Italy. Moodmakers include beamed darkwood ceilings, Renaissance paintings, and murals of Venice. Best of all, house specialties are not that expensive.

Kristofer's exudes the essence of the Mediterranean. Translation: There's water on the floor. Just kidding. This is a cozy little cafe with the emphasis on steaks and seafood. A nice touch is a complimentary crock of cheese with each entree. Desserts are special, including their famous Smoky Bon-Bons, served in a dazzling tableside display.

Rik' Shaw has a Far Eastern menu with over 100 entrees, including moo goo gai pan, char sue ding, and chow har kew. If you're not sure what you want, just point at something and nod sagely. "Ahh, here we are. Beef chow mein for the lady, soft-boiled coconut for the gentleman."

For snacks, try the Mardi Gras Food Court. In a Paris sidewalk setting, you have your choice of almost a dozen fast-food, ice cream, and pastry shops. Afterwards, you have your choice of bicarbonate of soda, Alka Seltzer, or Rolaids.

# Sahara

In the mid-1960s, the Strip was known for its three "S's"—the Sands, the Stardust, and the Sahara. The Sands is gone now, sunk but not forgotten. The Stardust is taking on water, but still managing to stay afloat. The Sahara almost capsized, but thanks to the genius (and money) of new owner William Bennett, it appears there's smooth sailing ahead for this Vegas landmark.

The Sahara Hotel was originally known as Club Bingo. It opened in 1947 across the road from the El Rancho Vegas with a couple of dice tables, a small entertainment lounge, and a 300-seat bingo parlor. Milton Prell, who later bought the Aladdin, took over the property five years later, remodeling it and renaming it the Sahara. Its nickname became "the Jewel of the Desert," and it gained a heady reputation for non-stop entertainment and hospitality. In fact, the Sahara's world-famous Congo Room played host to such stars as Mae West, Judy Garland, Johnny Carson, Marlene Dietrich, Tony Bennett, and Don Rickles. Esther Williams unveiled her supper club act at the Sahara shortly after it opened and George Burns was a regular during the sixties.

That was then. What about now? Well, Bennett (former head of the Circus Circus empire) has spent more than $100 million turning the Sahara into a Moroccan-themed paradise with stone columns, jeweled lattice work, gold ceilings, a harem-style swimming pool, and an eye-catching "onion" dome atop a glittering new entrance.

One of the Sahara's most popular attractions is the $15 million Sahara Speedworld, a virtual-reality Indy car race. Using motion hydraulics, wraparound screens, and a 16-channel sound system, you can actually feel the power of an 800-horsepower engine as you zip around the track in your own race car at speeds up to 220 miles an hour. Price: $8 for eight minutes and your choice of two different race tracks.

Restaurants include the Sahara Steak House, Paco's Hideaway Bar & Grill, the Caravan Room Coffee Shop, and the 40,000 square-foot Sahara Buffet that serves an estimated 8,000 people per day on weekends. (So eat there during the week.)

# Barbary Coast

When I first came to Las Vegas, there was a dinky little place called the Times Square Motel sitting on the corner of the Strip and Flamingo. It was on such a small sliver of land that no investor ever gave it a second thought. That is, not until Jackie and Michael Gaughan came along. Owners of a local gaming empire, they bought the property in 1979 and turned it into the Barbary Coast Hotel and Casino.

Every casino in town has to have something to separate it from its competition, and the Barbary Coast is no exception. Its claim to fame is being the "stained-glass capital of Las Vegas." Now that you're duly impressed, look around. You're literally surrounded by Tiffany-styled glass throughout the hotel. The most impressive stained-glass display is on the casino's west wall. Called "The Garden of Earthly Delights," this 30-foot piece of graffiti took 10 artists more than 10,000 man hours to complete, and is the largest mural of its kind in the world.

The Barbary Coast is small, jumbled, and noisy, but it does have a truly great gourmet restaurant called Michael's. The surroundings are part of the restaurant's charm, especially the stained-glass domed ceiling which arches over the entire room. Michael's features a magnificent menu of continental cuisine, appetizers, soups, salads, fresh vegetables, and fine wines. The perfect ending to a perfect meal is the assortment of fresh and chocolate-dipped fruits and after-dinner liqueurs. It's been voted Las Vegas' best restaurant, and I think it was also voted Las Vegas' most expensive restaurant.

# Harrah's

Across the Strip from Caesars Palace is Harrah's, the colorful flagship of the fleet founded by Nevada gaming pioneer Bill Harrah. Remodeled at a cost of $200 million, Harrah's has gone from a dinky riverboat theme to a jazzy carnival motif. Now there's a dramatic entryway adorned with dark glass and brilliant colors, nightly fireworks, a Brazilian-themed indoor-outdoor bar right on the Strip, a new 35-story tower that gives the hotel almost 2,400 rooms and suites, and a new porte cochere (which is French for front porch).

Actually, Harrah's could have saved most of that money just by opening the whole front of the joint to the street. After all, it's within a stone's throw of half a dozen other major casinos on the Vegas Strip. With 30,000 people walking past it every day, Harrah's would be a successful operation no matter what it looked like.

But now that the bulldozers and cranes are gone, you'll want to see Carnaval Court, a plaza area punctuated with decorative palms, a festive gazebo, and the free "Carnaval Fantastique" show four times nightly (dancers, acrobats, gymnasts). Or have a tropical drink at the fantasy beach lounge La Playa and watch the world go by outside your Strip-side window.

Restaurants at Harrah's include Asia, featuring enticing Asian cuisine; Cafe Andreotti, Italian food served in an outdoor Tuscan Hills-like atmosphere; and the Range Steakhouse, the first Las Vegas restaurant directly overlooking the Strip.

There's also the Fresh Market Square Buffet, with "action" cooking stations behind the serving lines; the Garden Cafe, for 24-hour service; Club Cappuccino, for specialty coffees and pastries; and Ghiradelli Chocolate Factory, featuring a chocolate shop and an old-fashioned soda fountain.

# Sands
## In Memoriam

Even though the Sands is closed now, it still belongs in this book. If it hadn't been for the Sands, I don't think Las Vegas would have ever achieved such international glitz and notoriety. To show you what I mean, let's roll back the clock to January 1960, when Frank Sinatra opened his "Summit Meeting at the Sands" with Dean Martin, Sammy Davis Jr., Peter Lawford, and Joey Bishop. The Rat Pack performed twice nightly for three weeks. During that time almost every big star in show business made a visit to the Sands, eventually winding up on stage and at the mercy of Sinatra and his clan. From Ralph Pearl's book, *Las Vegas Is My Beat*, here's what it was like:

*Frank Sinatra dashed over to a slightly bewildered Sammy Davis Jr. He picked him up bodily as though he were a bundle of laundry, then rushed to the mike. "Ladies and gentlemen," Frank said as he held up Sammy, "I want to thank all of you for giving me this valuable NAACP trophy." Then Sinatra, still carrying Davis in his arms, walked over to a prominent-looking gent at ringside and dropped his trophy in the man's lap. The prominent gent? None other than Senator John F. Kennedy of Massachusetts, already being touted for the White House. Davis looked up into Kennedy's face and meekly said, "It's perfectly all right with me, Senator, as long as I'm not being donated to George Wallace."*

*More howling as Joey Bishop and Peter Lawford retrieved Davis from Senator Kennedy, then disappeared out the door. Moments later they came back onstage without Sammy. Noticing their sad expressions, Frank and Dean asked, "What happened to the trophy?"*

*Joey Bishop: "We played it on the hard eight, and lost."*

After the show, everyone adjourned to the Winner's Circle Lounge to catch Louis Prima and Keely Smith, backed up by Sam Butera and the Witnesses. Sinatra and other Rat Packers might also hold court there, or they might deal a few hands of blackjack in the casino. "It was picnic time," Joey Bishop remembered. "That's all it was. It was just fun. We couldn't wait to go to work."

The Sands opened in December 1952 with 200 rooms and a snappy little logo: "A Place in the Sun." Built at a cost of $5.5 million by horse breeder Jakie Friedman, the Sands really owed its success to entertainment director Jack Entratter. Entratter, former owner of the Copacabana in New York, knew practically every celebrity on the planet, as well as most of the international press corps. He hired the stars for the Copa Room; he filled the audience with other stars; and he wined and dined famous columnists to write about all those stars—and about the Sands.

The result was one of the most magical periods in the history of Las Vegas. And it might have lasted forever—if Jakie Friedman hadn't died, and if Frank Sinatra hadn't quit after a big fight with the casino manager, and if time could have just stood still for a while. But it never does. Newer flashier casinos captured the public's fancy. In the end, the Sands was a 44-year-old eyesore.

It closed for good June 30, 1996, and the last play at the dice table that night was by Vegas hotshot Bob Stupak. "One more roll," he pleaded, minutes before the casino shut down. The dealer handed him the dice and he put $1,000 on the field. Stupak rolled a 5, losing his money, and the table was promptly closed. Interestingly, all the players who backed Bob on the pass line were allowed to pick up their bets. They probably didn't know it, but that gave them an 11% edge. Well, hey, no wonder the Sands had to close.

Owner Sheldon Adelson is in the process of building the $2 billion Venetian megaresort where the old Sands once stood. He even hints that "Sands" might be incorporated somewhere in the hotel's theme. It doesn't really matter, though. The real Sands will live on in our imaginations, and in our memories.

"...the most beautiful girls in the world, the famous Copa Girl..." "...a big round of applause for Mr. Humphrey Bogart and his lovely wife Lauren Bacall..." "...and now the Sands proudly presents..." "...Nat King Cole..." "...Tallulah Bankhead..." "...Milton Berle..." "...Red Skelton..." "...Marlene Dietrich..."

Adelson promises his new resort will be the biggest in the world, with 6,000 suites and a convention complex, surrounded by canals, gondolas, and lush foliage. I wish him luck. I also offer this suggestion. Put a little museum in that big building somewhere. Place all the memorabilia of the old Sands inside it. The old photos, and the old posters, and the old props. I guarantee it will be the most popular room in that $2 billion hotel.

# New Frontier

The other day a woman called the New Frontier. "What time is your buffet?" she asked.

"What time can you be here?" was the reply.

Well yes, things are a little slow at the New Frontier these days, but at one time this was the most elaborate casino in Las Vegas. A rambling ranch-style string of bungalows, it opened as the Last Frontier in late 1942 with a slogan that said it all: "The Early West in Modern Splendor." Back then, the only other things jumping on the old L.A. Highway were a couple of honky tonks, a filling station, and the El Rancho Vegas—which had opened 18 months earlier.

The Last Frontier, though, was pure magic. Movie stars would ride through the desert on horses from the hotel's stables, which photographers captured for newspapers around the country. The dinner show in the Last Frontier's elaborate showroom cost $3.50 a plate, with such stars on stage as Sophie Tucker and Judy Garland. But the greatest publicity the joint ever got was in 1956, when the hotel (by this time known as the New Frontier) gambled on an upcoming singer named Elvis Presley. Unfortunately, the type of tourist that Vegas attracted in those years wasn't the kind who listened to rock and roll on the radio, and Elvis' show turned out to be a dud.

So did the Last Frontier, for that matter. People were tiring of Western-style casinos, and by this time there were lots of new places around. In 1966, the hotel was bulldozed, reopening a year later as the New Frontier with a ten-story high-rise, and 650 deluxe rooms. It cost the owners $16 million, but still the property languished. One reason might be this story that appeared in a Las Vegas newspaper in 1967:

"The operating corporation has been in difficulties recently with local law enforcement agencies and the State Gaming Control Board. Sheriff Ralph Lamb raided a suite in the hotel about 10 days ago and arrested Tony Zerilli and other men from Detroit on a vagrancy charge. Lamb identified Zerilli as a son of Joe Zerilli, reported to be the Detroit head of Cosa Nostra."

That's when billionaire Howard Hughes rode to the rescue, offering $24 million for the property and changing its name to the Frontier. His Summa Corporation held onto it until 1988, when it was purchased by Margaret Elardi. The first thing she did was take out the Frontier's showroom. Then she incurred the wrath of unions across the country by refusing to sign a collective bargaining agreement with hotel union workers. Consequently, they went on strike—and stayed out for 6 years, 4 months, and 10 days.

Still, it worked out pretty well for Margaret. She paid $70 million for the place, and sold it in 1998 for $165 million. The new owner is Kansas industrialist Phil Ruffin, who immediately settled the strike and put everyone back to work. (He also changed the name back to the New Frontier.) The hotel, however, is sorely in need of some TLC. There are only four places to eat: Gold Rush Cafe, Michelle's Village Buffet, Phil's Angus Steakhouse, and Margarita's Mexican Cantina.

What's in the future? Look for the New Frontier to get a complete facelift. Gun maker Smith and Wesson is already negotiating with Ruffin to open a themed restaurant inside the hotel. And hopefully, that's just the beginning.

# Hard Rock

Who would have thought the day would come when a senior citizen's favorite song would be "Rock Around the Clock?" Rock 'n' roll music is a universal language today, and in keeping with that theme may we present the Hard Rock Hotel—for hard gambling, hard drinking and—er, hard rock.

A recent survey showed that eight of ten patrons rated the Hard Rock as "like awesome, man." So it comes as no surprise that this resort is really aimed toward a younger crowd. In fact, the average age of a Hard Rock customer is between 25 and 35. Fortunately for owner Peter Morton, this age group has more money than the average Vegas visitor. "And the bottom line is this," Morton says. "The 30-year-old yuppie who drives a BMW convertible and goes to a Bruce Springsteen concert loves to gamble." (The Hard Rock's showroom is called "The Joint," and recent concerts featured such rock legends as Bob Dylan, Steely Dan, and Elton John.)

The 11-story Hard Rock Hotel is located east of the Las Vegas Strip on Paradise Road. You'll have to take a cab, but it's worth the trip. There's rock 'n' roll paraphernalia everywhere, and I'm not talking roach clips. You'll see $2 million worth of authentic rock relics, such as Buddy Holly's monogrammed boots, Elvis Presley's gold lame jacket, Jimi Hendrix's flying V guitar, and even a Harley Davidson motorcycle from Guns N' Roses. (I'm no yuppie: I thought Guns N' Roses was a Russian vodka.)

Other Hard Rock oddities include roulette tables shaped like pianos, a chandelier made of saxophones, and gambling chips imprinted with classic rock logos. There's the $5 Red Hot Chili Pepper "Give It Away" chip, the $25 Jimi Hendrix "Purple Haze" chip, and the $100 Tom Petty "You Got Lucky" chip.

You don't get a key when you check in at the Hard

Rock. You get a "backstage pass." Simply hang it around your neck and you don't have to pay for anything! That is, until you check out. This can get expensive, because room prices start at $75 on weekdays and can range as high as $300 on weekends. Got an extra person in your party? That'll be another $25. One neat room feature, though, is the French windows that actually open so you can get some fresh air. I also like the unique "Do Not Disturb" signs. At Hard Rock, the signs read, "I Hear You Knockin' But You Can't Come In." Okay, for that I'll pay $300, but I get to keep the sign, right?

**CASINO SECRET**

Casinos love it when you take home a commemorative or personalized gaming chip as a souvenir. They cost the casinos about 45¢ apiece.

The Hard Rock is probably the most environment-friendly resort in Vegas. All printed materials are on recycled paper with soy-based inks. All glass, aluminum, steel, and paper products are recycled. The housekeeping staff uses only non-toxic biodegradable cleaning products. Leftover foods go to the homeless. And get this: the profits from one bank of slot machines go to save the rain forests. (Profits from the other 798 slots go to save the Hard Rock.)

Restaurants include the world-famous Hard Rock Cafe next door; Mortoni's for food with an Italian twist; and Mr. Lucky's, a 24-hour coffee shop. By the way, the restaurants use only natural ingredients, including organic produce and vegetarian alternatives.

Now that you've eaten, drank, and gambled your day

away at the Hard Rock, there's only one thing left to do. Everybody on the dance floor!

"One, two, three o'clock, four o'clock rock…five, six, seven o'clock, eight o'clock rock…nine, ten, eleven o'clock, twelve o'clock rock…"

# Mandalay Bay
## (Opening in 1999)

Imagine a fabled city where caravans from East and West converge, spilling out a wealth of luxurious and exotic wares from far-flung empires. Imagine exotic drinks and sandy beaches, viewed from private cabanas under swaying palm trees. Now imagine you and your friends enjoying all this, in a place called Mandalay Bay. Why, you can almost hear the tom toms in the distance. Oh, wait a minute. Those weren't tom toms. It was just a tourist with 18 ashtrays in her purse.

Built by Circus Circus Enterprises, Mandalay Bay is located south of Luxor on the site of the old Hacienda Hotel. What makes this luxury resort so unique is its hotel-within-a-hotel concept. You can either stay at Mandalay Bay or check in at the Four Seasons—which has its own five floors of five-star accommodations near the top of the Mandalay Bay towers.

By day, wile away your hours at a 10-acre sandy-beach pool area. Other water attractions include a 3/4-mile lazy river, a surfing wave beach, a snorkeling reef, and a swim-up shark tank. Then head to the giant 30,000-square-foot spa for a steam bath and rubdown.

Mandalay Bay's approach to entertainment assumes most of us would rather have a great meal than see a great show. Consequently, a dozen restaurants are in the works, including one that will overlook a swan-filled lagoon down on the beach. Other options include the Marketplace Buffet, the All Day Cafe, and an on-site rum distillery.

| | |
|---|---|
| **Cost:** | $950 million |
| **Rooms:** | 3,700 |
| **Size:** | 43 floors |
| **Entertainment:** | A 12,000-seat major events arena, showroom, and lounges. |

**Casino:**          110,000 square feet with special facilities for high-end players.

**Conventions:**     Approximately 100,000 square feet at Mandalay Bay and 20,000 square feet at Four Seasons.

# Alexis Park

This is one of the most unusual resorts in Las Vegas. Located off the Strip on Harmon Avenue, Alexis Park is a favorite hideaway of the rich and famous, and it offers something no other resort offers. Or rather, it doesn't offer something all the others do. There's no gambling here!

That cuts the crowds down considerably, and frankly that's what's so nice about Alexis Park. You're in a dreamy setting of greenery, streams, and waterfalls, and you don't have to worry about getting trampled to death by a mob of check-cashing, cup-clutching, camera-clicking commoners.

It's on the expensive side, but Alexis Park does offer special packages from time to time, which drop the rate on a luxury suite to $99 a night. If you want to go first class, get a suite with jacuzzi and fireplace. Your room price includes a complete breakfast, complimentary newspaper, and use of the health spa, three pools, lighted tennis courts, and nine-hole putting green.

Alexis Park is also home to the award-winning Pegasus restaurant. Gourmet dining with special menus on request. Among those who have eaten here are Dustin Hoffman, Tom Cruise, Whitney Houston, Charlton Heston, and Dan Quayle.

Alexis Park is one of the best-kept secrets in Las Vegas. Keep it that way.

Sshhh.

# Paris
## (Opening in 1999)

Well, it had to happen. Paris was home to the world-famous Eiffel Tower, and Las Vegas wanted it. So early in 1998, a group of American mercenaries—led by Las Vegas Mayor Jan Jones—slipped into the French capital and began the arduous task of secretly dismantling the tower piece by piece. The pieces were then smuggled out of Orly Airport in suitcases, and reassembled on a 24-acre piece of land next door to Bally's on the Las Vegas Strip.

The result will be one of Las Vegas' most glittering resorts—and war with France, which now wants the Statue of Liberty back.(Ironically, that's in Las Vegas, too, at New York-New York.)

The Hilton Corporation, which also owns Bally's, inherited the 34-story Paris, which will have 2,914 rooms, 300 suites, nine restaurants, five bars, a showroom, a European health spa, a two-acre rooftop swimming pool, lighted tennis courts, and a wedding chapel.

In addition to a 50-story scale model of the Eiffel Tower, the resort also features replicas of other French landmarks, including the Arc de Triomphe, the Paris Opera House, and the Louvre. There's even a recreation of a Paris metro station that will connect to the monorail linking Bally's and the MGM Grand.

Dining facilities include:

Eiffel Tower, a French restaurant inside the mezzanine of the Paris landmark.

Rotisserie, a two-level cafe where meats are roasted over flames.

Brasserie, an outdoor restaurant-bar.

Cafe, a coffee shop featuring European coffees and homemade breads.

Le Provencal, an informal Italian-style restaurant with an open kitchen.

The Village Buffet, specializing in classic foods from the five French provinces. Seating at the buffet is arranged in a village-like setting, where you can either eat in the town square on inside a French country home.

There's also one bar that I've just got to mention: Napoleon's Retreat. The name alone should make it a success, but just in case, it also features a cigar lounge, live entertainment, hot and cold French appetizers, French wines by the glass, and a good selection of microbrewery and imported beers.

Viva la France!

**CASINO SECRET**

For a great view of the Strip, go to the observation deck of the Eiffel Tower, which will be the second-highest structure in the city.

# Vacation Village

For bargain hunters, Vacation Village is worth the drive (southern end of the Las Vegas Strip). Buy $10 worth of nickels or quarters at the front bar anytime, and get a free hot dog and beer. The secret is to put the $10 back in your pocket after you eat. Show your airline ticket within 12 hours of arrival and get a free spin on the Money Wheel. You're a guaranteed winner of anything from a dollar in quarters to a suite for two nights or even $400 in airfare reimbursement.

Vacation Village promotes heavily with free drawings, low buy-in "bingo parties," and other creative giveaways that are worth checking into.

# Stratosphere

You've left the glittering Las Vegas Strip, and now you're on your way downtown. See that huge tower over there on the left? That's the Stratosphere. Pull in, you're gonna love this place!

It used to be called Bob Stupak's Vegas World, and though most people considered it the biggest joke in town, it was actually a great place for gamblers. Stupak loved to splash full-page ads in national magazines and Sunday supplementals. He offered unlimited drinks, free show tickets, free meals, a free spin on his money wheel, free keno tickets, $300 worth of chips for a $300 room package, and all kinds of other giveaways. This deal, known as the VIP Vacation, was the longest running, most successful, and most misunderstood promotion in Las Vegas history. Because it was gambling intensive, a lot of people didn't know how to take advantage of it. Those who did loved it, and took Stupak up on his offers time after time.

Then Stupak got an even bigger idea. Why not build a huge sign high in the air to ballyhoo his paradise? Better yet, what about a giant tower! The Las Vegas City Council finally gave him permission, and in 1991 Stupak began to build his dream. But he ran into problems from the get-go. Mushrooming costs, a flash fire at 500 feet, and worst of all, the ugly cement tower was becoming the butt of everyone's jokes. In fact, I even came up with one myself. "You've heard of the Eiffel Tower? Well, this is the Awful Tower."

Broke and disgusted, Stupak turned to poker buddy Lyle Berman for help. Berman, the head of Grand Casinos, sunk enough money into the property to wind up with a controlling interest. The Stupak Tower became the Stratosphere, and at 1,149 feet (or 112 stories), it is now the highest free-standing observatory in the U.S. and the tallest building west of the Mississippi. Of course, this causes problems for airplanes leaving McCarran Airport. "This is flight 234. We're presently at 1,148 feet, and we should—uh oh!!" Just kidding. The tower is only on emergency flight paths.

Under the shiny wraps of Grand Casinos, however, the Stratosphere has finally taken on respect and public trust. And with a revolving restaurant, two observation decks, and a gravity-defying ride, the Stratosphere has become a popular tourist destination. Standard rooms start at just $69.

For panoramic views of the Strip and Las Vegas Valley, go to the observation decks in the tower's 12-level pod. The Pepsi-Cola indoor observation deck is on Level 8; the outdoor deck is on Level 9. Nothing is really free in this world, and the view from on high will cost you $5 ($4 with a Nevada driver's license).

**Ride the world's highest thrill rides.** On Level 12 (at 909 feet) is the High Roller. It's the highest roller coaster in the world, but doesn't live up to expectations. If you're craving real excitement, forget the High Roller and take a spin in my 1987 Hyundai.

The Big Shot is perched one floor higher. You're rocketed 160 feet into the air along a mast atop the tower's needle, then you free-fall back to the launching pad. Reaching speeds of 45 miles an hour on the way up, the Big Shot is a helluva thrill. Cost: $5. Chicken out at the last minute, and get all your money back.

Restaurants at the Stratosphere include Roxy's Dinner, another '50s place with old-fashioned burgers and shakes; Big Sky, with Western-style barbecue; Sister's Cafe & Grille, with 24-hour sandwiches and steaks; and Ferraro's, an annex of one of the most popular Italian restaurants in Vegas, with great Colorado lamb chops and house specialty Osso Buco.

Where you really want to go is the Top of the World Restaurant and Lounge, found on Level 6 in the tower. The restaurant does a complete 360-degree revolution every 80 minutes or so, which means you get a different view every time you look out the window.

I know it sounds romantic, but sometimes it can be embarrassing. A friend of mine left his table to go to the bathroom, then couldn't find his way back again. "Let's see, my window was looking out at the Sahara Hotel, so here we go. Oh, excuse me, folks, but I think you're sitting at my table. AND WHICH ONE OF YOU ATE MY PORK CHOPS?"

The food at the Top of the World Restaurant is contemporary, with prime rib, fresh fish, and Chocolate Stratosphere dessert. Prices range from around $10 for lunch to around $30 for dinner. Reservations are a must; otherwise, you'll have to pay $5 to get up to the restaurant.

# 13
# Downtown Las Vegas

Downtown Las Vegas is the home of the most photographed four blocks in the world. This is where it all started in 1931, when gambling was legalized in the state of Nevada. One of the oldest building sites in town is the Las Vegas Club, which opened as the Overland Park Hotel in 1905. A fire later burned the Overland to the ground, mainly because there wasn't enough water pressure to put the darn thing out. Then the Golden Gate opened, originally as the Hotel Nevada and later as the Sal Sagev. (Say it backwards.)

Where the Coin Castle stands today was the original location of the Northern Club, the first legal casino in the United States. Its proprietor was Lon Groesbeck of the Salt Lake City Brewing Company, who made a fortune selling American Beauty Beer for a nickel a glass. Unfortunately for Mr. Groesbeck, he was doing it during Prohibition.

By the mid-1930s, Fremont Street was paved, there was one traffic light, and the Union Pacific Depot was running five passenger trains a day from Los Angeles. The most popular night spot at the time on Fremont Street was the Barrel House Beer Garden, with a full orchestra and dancing every evening. There was a hole cut in the wall connecting it to the State Cafe next door, through which patrons could order food and whiskey. Who knows, this could have been the first "hole in the wall" gang.

What really put the city on the map was World War II. The Army built an air force training base outside of town, and homesick GIs were soon filling every saloon and casino in sight. By this time, Fremont Street was graced by such splendid dens of iniquity as the Apache Hotel (now the oldest part of the Horseshoe), the Pioneer Club, and the Monte Carlo Club. Just after the war ended, the Golden Nugget opened. This, by the way, was the first Las Vegas structure designed from the ground up to actually be a casino. The rest of them started out as bars or hotels.

But the blossoming of the Las Vegas Strip, starting with the opening of the El Rancho Vegas in 1941, sent the historic downtown area into an uncontrolled tailspin, and until late 1995, things didn't improved much. A survey of visitors who didn't visit downtown showed that 38% didn't have time, 24% weren't interested, 8% said it was inconvenient, and 7% said they didn't like the area. The neon-splashed Glitter Gulch of the '40s, that marvelous devilish avenue we saw in so many old movies, had evolved into a hangout for people down on their luck, and those who just couldn't afford to go anywhere else.

Because of this, downtown had a certain sleaziness about it that had you checking your valuables every time somebody bumped into you. Beyond the bright lights of Fremont Street, derelicts weaved along the sidewalks, and you moved with your head down, avoiding eye contact and walking a little bit faster than normal. Why, there's even a topless joint right in the middle of the block.

Downtown merchants tossed a few ideas around in an attempt to bring the magic back. One was a plan to turn Fremont Street into a canal, with everyone being ferried to the different casinos by gondolas. Then someone came up with the idea of a Star Trek attraction, where a life-sized replica of the Starship Enterprise would be parked at the corner of Fremont Street and Las Vegas Boulevard. But the idea that everyone finally agreed on was the $70 million Fremont Street Experience. The Fremont Street Experience has transformed four blocks of Fremont Street into a light and sound show unlike any you've ever seen. The street itself has been closed to vehicular traffic, and it's been enhanced with palm trees and cobblestone walkways. There's a kind of comfortable indoors feeling about it, which is especially nice on a hot summer or cold winter night.

The focal point is overhead, where giant columns support a space frame, 90 feet high at its peak and nearly 1,500 feet in length. Set into the inner surface of the space frame are 2.1 million lights that come to life during each show. Programmed by 32 computers, the lights create vivid animated images, synchronized with music and sound. The result is the colorful Fremont Street Experience that seems to come galloping right at you. To make it even more impressive, all the fabled neon lights of Glitter Gulch are switched off at the same instant just before the show so there are no distractions.

The only drawback to the Fremont Street Experience is that thousands of other people are there to see it, too, and it's best to be directly under the space frame in order to get the show's full impact. So you might not be too comfortable, standing there with your head tilted back and your hand on your wallet. Still, it's a great show, and it's free. Shows start at dusk, and run every hour on the hour. Each show lasts about seven minutes.

Major casinos downtown include Las Vegas Club, Fitzgeralds, California, Fremont, Lady Luck, Four Queens, Jackie Gaughan's Plaza, Golden Gate, El Cortez, Golden Nugget, and Binion's Horseshoe. You can spend hours wandering from one to another, so let's save time—here are the ones you'll want to see.

# Golden Nugget

Steve Wynn's Golden Nugget was his second Las Vegas acquisition. The first was a small strip of land butting up against the sound end of Caesars Palace. The land, which was leased from the Summa Corporation, was being used as a parking lot by Caesars. Wynn, a liquor distributor at the time, borrowed $1 million and bought the land from Summa. Then he turned around and sold it to Caesars for $2 million. And just like that, Wynn became a millionaire. He took the money and invested it in the Golden Nugget, and by 1972 he was chairman of the board. Still not satisfied, he borrowed another $60 million to give the Nugget a completely new look. The result is an absolutely gorgeous hotel that would hold its own right alongside his new Bellagio.

The gleaming gold and white design outside, with tiny white lights and graceful umbrella canopies, sets the Golden Nugget worlds apart from the flashy neon tubing elsewhere along Fremont. Swaying palm trees line the front like giant exclamation marks. There's a gentle glow about it all that lures you right into the casino.

Originally, that's all the Golden Nugget was—a gambling hall, with no rooms at all. Today the Nugget has almost 2,000 rooms and suites, five restaurants, a health spa, and a central-courtyard pool area with computerized misting systems. Throughout the hotel are imported marble floors and hand-engraved glass doors that give the whole place a heavy touch of European elegance.

The Golden Nugget has one of the classiest buffets in town. It's called, simply, The Buffet. There's also the Carson Street Cafe for 24-hour service, the California Pizza Kitchen, Lillie Langtry's for Chinese food, and Stefano's for Italian fare.

Before you leave, look for the special display of gold nuggets. The showcase near the main casino gives you a close-up look at 28 pieces of pure raw gold, including the largest single nugget in the world. It's called "The Hand of Faith" and weighs a massive 61 pounds, 11 ounces. Believe it or not, the huge nugget was found by an Australian in his own backyard. He didn't even have to dig for it; it was just sticking out of the ground.

Excuse me a minute while I take a little walk in my backyard.

# Binion's Horseshoe

Binion's Horseshoe is named for its founder, Benny Binion—a cowboy turned gambler who rolled into Vegas in a Cadillac limousine back in 1946. All he brought with him were a few dreams, some tattered memories, and $2 million in cash. The old man died in 1989, but his world-famous Binion's Horseshoe lives on.

The Horseshoe is a pure gambling joint. Benny Binion's rule was simple: a man's first bet was his limit. That's still the case. It backfired on him a few times, but in the long run he wound up with most of the chips. A man named Murphy once strode into the Horseshoe with $15 million in cash. He wanted to play craps. Binion's son Jack (now president of the Horseshoe) asked his dad, "What if he wants to bet a million dollars a pop?"

"Well, we'll try 'em a few rolls," Binion grinned. "We can quit anytime we want to."

I spent two days interviewing Binion shortly before his death, and I asked him what it was that made the Horseshoe such a successful operation. His answer:

"We treat people with courtesy. Feed 'em good. Good whiskey. Cheap. Give 'em a good gamble. And that's all there is to it, son."

You can still get good food and good whiskey, cheap. Beer and well drinks are only a dollar at any casino bar, and that keeps the glasses hoisted morning, noon, and night. I remember once when my cousin Alex came to visit. We plopped ourselves down at a Horseshoe bar and ordered a couple of drinks. Alex paid for the round with a $10 bill. The bartender gave him back $8. "I think you made a mistake," Alex said to him. He thought he got too much change back, but he hadn't. And just like that the Horseshoe had itself a brand new customer.

The Horseshoe has two of the best restaurants downtown, and believe it or not one of them is the coffee shop! The Binion's Horseshoe coffee shop serves up some hon-

est homestyle cooking, with a $2.75 breakfast, great bar-
becued chicken, and Benny Binion's special Texas Horseshoe chili. The coffee shop also has one of the best bargains
in town—a big steak with all the trimmings for just $4.

Twenty-four floors up, atop the hotel tower is Binion's
Ranch Steakhouse. (Take the outdoor glass elevator.) The
specialty of the house is a 20-ounce porterhouse, slowly
cooked over a mesquite-charcoal open-pit broiler. The
stained glass over the bar comes from the original
steakhouse restaurant built back in the 1950s. Great food,
great view, great service. Reservations suggested.

Binion's Horseshoe is also home to the annual World
Series of Poker, the largest and longest-running poker
tournament in the world. In the championship event, each
player buys in for $10,000 and the winner gets a million
dollars. The entire tournament lasts about three weeks,
from the middle of April to the first week in May. The
final showdown attracts a huge crowd and is worth
watching from the sidelines, as the world's best poker
players go heads-up against one another. The atmosphere
is electric, the action is riveting, and you can feel the ten-
sion mounting as hundreds of thousands of dollars
change hands on the turn of a single card.

The tournament started with just two players back
in 1949. One of the world's most renowned gamblers at
the time was a man named Nicholas Dondolos, better
known as "Nick the Greek." The Greek approached
Benny Binion with an unusual request: set him up in a
high-stakes poker game against the best poker player
around, which happened to be a brash young friend of
Binion's named Johnny Moss. Benny agreed to do it, but
under one condition. The game had to be played in public view at Binion's Horseshoe Club.

During the marathon, which lasted five months, Moss
and Dondolos played every form of poker imaginable.
"We played and played, and I beat him at every game,"
Moss told me years later. "I was the best draw poker

player there was, best deuce to seven player, the top stud player, and the best there ever was playing hold 'em.'"

Moss ultimately won the big game, along with an estimated $2 million. When Nick the Greek lost his last pot, he rose, bowed slightly, and uttered these now-famous words, "Mr. Moss, I have to let you go."

(See the Poker Hall of Fame with great pics of Johnny Moss and other legendary card sharks. It's located on the wall in the main casino.)

You may not win a million dollars playing poker at Binion's Horseshoe, but at least you can look at a million dollars up close. The Million Dollar Display is located near the stairs leading to the coffee shop. Encased behind bullet-proof glass in a giant horseshoe, the display is comprised of a hundred $10,000 bills. Binion claimed he bought the bills from banks. Others say he won the money from a Texas oilman.

Incidentally, Benny Binion put that million dollars on display in 1954. I was trying to figure out how much that money would be worth today if he had stuck it in a bank and let the interest accumulate at an average of 5% over a period of roughly 45 years. I couldn't do it, so I turned for help to a Las Vegas schoolteacher and her first-grade class. Here are their tabulations. One million times point oh-five times 45 equals…and there's a great big picture of a purple dinosaur. That looks nice, kids.

**CASINO SECRET** Binion's Million Dollar Display is worth seeing, and you can get your picture taken in front of it. The color photo is given to you on the spot (no two hour wait while you feed the slot machines). It's the best possible memento of your Vegas vacation—and it's free!

# Four Queens

Remember when "my dad could beat your dad?" Well, the Four Queens has some bragging rights of its own. It has the largest slot machine in the world, the biggest blackjack table in the world, and probably the best gourmet restaurant in the city.

Built in 1964, the Four Queens started out as a pint-sized property with 120 rooms and a mouse-hole casino. How it got its catchy name is simple enough to explain. You see, owner Ben Goffstein had four daughters: Faith, Hope, Benita, and Michelle.

Over the years, the Four Queens (now owned by the Elsinore Group) has grown in size and stature. It has also become a big-time slot sanctuary with 175,000 members in its Reel Winners Club and 30,000 members in its Club 55, one of the few casino clubs for seniors. (Pretty soon there'll be slot machines that take Social Security checks.)

**Check out the world's largest slot machine.** Listed in the Guinness Book of World Records, the Queen's Machine is almost 10 feet high and nearly 18 feet long. It can be played simultaneously by six people who have a chance to win up to $50,000, and a much better chance to lose every dime they have to their name.

**Play at the world's largest blackjack table.** It seats 12 players and requires two dealers. The table is four feet deep by 11 feet long, uses 27,864 inches of plywood, 16,496 inches of Formica, 864 inches of vinyl, and 6,408 inches of felt. I know, because I measured it the other night.

**Eat at Hugo's Cellar.** I've never heard a bad word said about this gourmet restaurant. When a lady is seated, she is presented with a beautiful long-stemmed rose. (They gave my mother-in-law a snapdragon.) Dinner begins with breads and cheese. Then comes your salad served tableside. Now an "intermezzo": raspberry sorbet in a miniature ice cream cone. This is to cleanse your wallet, I think they told me. Now comes your entree. This is followed by chocolate-dipped fruits served with fresh whipped cream.

But wait, you're not finished yet. There's a pastry cart and after-dinner liqueurs, and the house specialty, which is Kona coffee prepared in a glass bubble at the table and sweetened with chocolate chips and whipped cream. If you're on an expense account, try the sampler appetizer for two: beef, swordfish, chicken, and shrimp cooked on a sizzling granite slab tableside. At any rate, say goodbye to that $100 bill hidden behind your driver's license. Hugo's Cellar is expensive.

# Fremont

It was 1956. "Heartbreak Hotel" was blasting on the jukebox, Hopalong Cassidy was grand marshal of the annual Helldorado Parade, and the Fremont Hotel in downtown Las Vegas opened its doors for the first time. Named for Fremont Street, which was named for explorer John Fremont, the Fremont was built at a grand cost of $6 million. It was also called Levinson's Folly, because everybody thought owner Ed Levinson was crazy to build a 15-story casino downtown when all the action was on the Strip.

Maybe they were right. Even though the Fremont Hotel was the site of many firsts (first Wayne Newton show, first above-ground swimming pool, first all-female-dealer card room), it just couldn't fly straight, finally crashing into Mount Foreclosure in 1984. It was taken over by the Boyd Group, and re-opened the next day. Since then more than $30 million has been poured into the property to give it back its old-time charm.

Restaurant row includes three nice eating rooms. Second Street Grill serves American cuisine with a Pacific rim influence; it's one of the best unknown restaurants in town. Tony Roma's has great barbecue and a nice bar. For a relaxed patio atmosphere, there's the Lanai Cafe that features a good Chinese menu and round-the-clock specials. For snacks, the Lanai Express Snack Bar has hot dogs, chili, beverages and the ever-popular Vegas shrimp cocktail that's worlds apart—a part shrimp, a part sauce, and two parts lettuce.

# Las Vegas Club

If you wander inside the Las Vegas Club downtown and see some stranger drinking Budweiser out of a long-neck, it just might be me. I like the Las Vegas Club. It reminds me of what Las Vegas used to be like before all these newfangled theme resorts got so popular. Actually, you may not know this, but the Las Vegas Club was the first themed hotel-casino in town—here the focus has always been on sports trivia. (The coffee shop is even called The Dugout.)

Las Vegas Club's Sports Hall of Fame features the most complete collection of baseball memorabilia this side of Cooperstown. You've got your World Series bat collection (1946-1958), you've got your autographed baseballs, you've got your old-time photos, and many other rare items. The Hall of Fame is a nice relaxing way to spend a few minutes, and it's free.

Steeped in history, the Las Vegas Club sits on the site of the oldest building in town. This is where Las Vegas started in 1905. Over the years, as gambling and tourism grew, so did the Las Vegas Club. And it's even bigger today. A second 16-story tower was recently added, which doubled the size of the hotel. Extra touches like soundproof rooms and security guards posted at the room elevators help the Las Vegas Club hold onto its reputation as *Las Vegas' best kept secret.*

For a romantic evening, have dinner in the Great Moments Room. This quiet little restaurant and lounge offers up some great gourmet dining at low, low prices. And I'll be darned if the maître d' didn't remember my name from TWO MONTHS EARLIER! That's when my wife whispered to me, "Honey, you're not at work now. Take off your name tag."

The Las Vegas Club boasts that it has the most liberal non-single-deck blackjack rules in the world. You can double down on your first two or three cards; double down on any two cards, any time you choose; split and re-split aces up to three times; split and re-split any other pair anytime; six cards totaling 21 or less automatically wins. Drawback: Six decks are used, dealer hits a soft 17, and with all these rules it's tough to play the strategy for them correctly.

# Fitzgeralds

Fitzgeralds Hotel and Casino opened on St. Patrick's Day in 1988. Sure, and what else would you be expectin'? It's big by downtown standards, with 650 rooms and a 10-story parking garage. Depending on the season and day of the week, you can get a room at Fitzgeralds for anywhere from $36 to $56 a night.

A nice touch at Fitzgeralds is the Rainbow's End Casino, where you can see money growing on trees, rub mascot Mr. O'Lucky's head for luck, and maybe spot a leprechaun peekin' from behind a shamrock. Oh, sorry, Mr. Rooney.

There's a good restaurant at Fitzgeralds called Limerick's, which serves up great steaks and seafood at bargain prices. The coffee shop is called Molly's Country Kitchen, which doubles as the buffet. What I like about Fitzgeralds is the fact that you get treated like a VIP. The top priority of each employee is to make sure your visit is a friendly and enjoyable one—or else! They call it the Fitzgeralds Experience, not to be confused with the Fremont Street Experience.

# Lady Luck

Located one block from Glitter Gulch on North Third Street downtown, the Lady Luck Hotel-Casino was listed number one in a recent *Las Vegas Advisor* survey as having the best of 60 Las Vegas prime rib meal deals: $4.49 for a regular cut, $8.99 for a king-sized cut, and $12.99 for the whole cow. The $8.99 slab is the best of the three for value. This special is good from 4 to 11 nightly in the Winner's Cafe.

European dining at domestic prices makes Lady Luck's Burgundy Room a popular local favorite. Prices range from $12.95 up to $33.95, and each entree comes with a nice seafood salad. Decor touches include hand-signed paintings by Salvador Dali and original statues from pre-war Paris.

If you play dollar slots or gamble $25 to $50 per hand, you'll get the royal treatment at Lady Luck by joining the Lady Luck "Mad Money Slot Club." Even mid-range players get full comps, including free suites, limo service, and use of the casino's private box for sporting events at Thomas and Mack Arena.

**CASINO SECRET** If you're from out of state and have never been rated at Lady Luck, call an executive host for a free VIP tour of the hotel. They'll even send a limo to pick you up. The whole tour takes about an hour, and for once in your life you'll be treated like royalty.

# The Rest of Downtown

The **Golden Gate** lays claim to being the oldest continuous operating hotel in Las Vegas, having opened in 1906 and passing through several different owners and names before taking on a San Francisco flavor in 1959. That year, the Gate started dishing up six-ounce shrimp cocktails a la Fisherman's Wharf, and it's been serving them ever since. Almost 40 years of shrimp cocktails have added up to nearly 30 million pounds of the crunchy little crustaceans, and though the price was raised a few years back, a cocktail glassful today is only 99¢. It's the best snack in town.

**Jackie Gaughan's Plaza** faces Fremont Street across Main, and has anchored Glitter Gulch since it was built in 1970. Its Centerstage Restaurant, in a glass dome on the second floor, looks right down the middle of the downtown casino core. With such a view, Jackie Gaughan, the last elder statesman of Las Vegas (he arrived in the 1940s), could really jack up the Centerstage prices, but he doesn't; all the menu items are reasonably priced. The Plaza is also known for its bank of penny slot machines and its Amtrak station, the only railroad depot in the country attached to a casino. Greyhound also gets into the act next door.

Jackie Gaughan also owns the **El Cortez** and **Gold Spike** a few blocks away. The El Cortez has what's generally believed to be the country's oldest existing casino wing, which was built in 1941 and has changed very little since. (It even seems like some of the customers came with the place.) Like the Centerstage, the steakhouse at El Cortez, Roberta's, serves good hearty steaks, seafood, and prime rib dinners for a song. Rooms here, as well as at the Gold Spike, are some of the least expensive around. The Gold Spike's rooms go for $20 a night 365 nights a year. The Gold Spike has another unique feature: a bank of penny video poker machines located in a section of the casino known as the "Copper Mine."

The **California** is the most inappropriately named casino in town, since it caters to an almost exclusively Hawaiian crowd. The carpet sports tropical flowers, the dealers wear Hawaiian shirts, the snack bars serve classic kau kau wagon plate lunches, and the islanders often get together in the lounges over ukeleles—you can almost smell the ocean. The California has one of the great downtown bargain restaurants, Pasta Pirate. The Redwood Bar and Grille steakhouse serves a huge porterhouse special that comes with dessert for $12.95.

The California's sister casino across Main Street is called, appropriately enough, **Main Street Station**. This casino had an illustrious, though very short, run in 1992, opening and closing in a mere eight months. It wasn't for lack of trying, though—it was a classy joint, full of antiques and fine touches (like a chunk of the Berlin Wall on display in the men's bathroom). It just had a few little financial problems. But it reopened in late 1996, complete with refurbished hotel rooms, an expanded casino, downtown's largest buffet and only microbrewery, and all the antiques intact. If anything, Main Street Station is even classier now than it was when it first opened.

# 14
# Neighborhood Casinos

A friend of mine once visited a plush Strip casino. He handed the bartender a $5 bill and asked for change. "Buddy," the bartender told him, "that *is* change."

Well, your trip to Las Vegas doesn't have to be like that. In fact, here is the biggest casino secret in this book: Sightsee in the fancy places. Stay in one if you like. Live it up; you've earned it. But spend some time in a neighborhood casino, or "locals joint," as residents call them. You're 15 minutes from one no matter where you stay in Vegas, and the money you save will make this one of the highlights of your whole trip.

These are the casinos where the locals go for looser slots, cheaper meals, small-town hospitality, and convenient access. After all, how can Palace Station compete with the Mirage or the MGM Grand? Palace Station gives away a *house* in its pro football contest, that's how—and it plies its customers with 99¢ margaritas, a free-wheeling slot club, and a dirt-cheap buffet.

The other locals joints take similar measures to get your business. Read on, and you'll see what I mean.

# Palace Station

Without a doubt, Palace Station is the most popular casino in Las Vegas for locals. It was one of the first casinos to spring up in a suburban area and cater to the built-in customer base provided by the surrounding neighborhoods. At the time everything else was either downtown, on the Strip, or out on Boulder Highway. Palace Station (then known as "the Casino") revolutionized the gaming industry when it opened at West Sahara near the off ramp of Interstate 15. Three years later the name was changed to Bingo Palace, and in 1984 it became Palace Station.

Today you can find casinos in practically every neighborhood in town, but none compares with this one. It has one of the best race and sports books anywhere, a 10,000-square-foot facility with 250 seats, along with 40 monitors and big screen TVs. There's also Palace Station's "Great Giveaway," which is probably the best pro football contest in town. What makes this tournament different is that not only do the contestants with the best season records win prizes, but also those with the worst records. In fact, one year a retired bartender won a brand new house after picking 157 losers in 212 games. Of course, he had to pay taxes on it—which wound up costing him $35,000. Oh well, into each life a little rain must fall. Hopefully, though, it's not coming through the roof!

In keeping with its railroad image, you'll find authentic-looking railroad cars both outside and inside. Palace Station's slot club is even called the "Boarding Pass Club." Like all the other slot clubs in town, you can qualify for rooms and meals just by cranking those handles. I saw a miracle take place at a Palace Station slot machine. A man hit a royal flush on a dollar machine, then walked away— *leaving his cane behind.*

What I really like about Palace Station are the restaurants. The food is excellent, and the prices are reasonable.

Eat till you drop in Palace Station's completely renovated gourmet buffet. The food is cooked right before your eyes, and last time I was there the cook was grilling 16-ounce sirloin steaks. There's even a separate dessert and flambé station. Open for breakfast, lunch, and dinner.

The Guadalajara Bar & Grille serves up authentic Mexican and Tex-Mex cuisine, with specialties that include shrimp Guadalajara and crabmeat enchiladas. Their 99¢ margarita has the whole town buzzing.

Everything from light fare to full-course dinners is on the menu at the 24-hour Iron Horse Cafe. A popular morning item is the skillet breakfast with three eggs, home fries, choice of meats, and all the pancakes and toast you can choke down.

Pasta Palace offers everything from spaghetti and meatballs to shrimp scampi and veal, prepared a variety of ways. Great pizza, too, cooked in a wood-burning oven.

My favorite, with a California coastal atmosphere and a fresh seafood salad bar, is the Broiler. Seafood and steaks are mesquite-grilled, and for the price you can't beat it.

Outside the Broiler is a cozy 16-seat oyster bar, where you can watch the chef prepare cioppino, bouillabaisse, shrimp loaf, oysters on the half shell, steamed clams, or other specialties—with nothing on the menu over $14. On one of my outings there, I overheard a woman customer tell the chef, "You have nice mussels today."

"Thanks," he said. "I've been lifting weights."

# Rio

The Rio, with a striking blue and red facade, is located at the corner of West Flamingo and Valley View Boulevard, and the dazzling marquee in front is a story in itself. At 125 feet high, the sign has nearly 13,000 feet of neon tubing and more than 5,000 light bulbs. Two gigantic maracas shake constantly among a cluster of sheet-metal leaves and fiberglass-confetti strands. The lights change continuously, practically hypnotizing you. (Not the marquee lights, the traffic lights at the intersection. C'mon, move it, butthead!)

The Rio has been voted one of the best hotels in Vegas. It's definitely worth seeing, if you don't mind leaving the Strip for a few hours and mingling with the locals.

Actually, the Rio got off to a shaky start when it opened in 1990. Since it was off the Strip, nobody from out of town even knew about it, and locals shunned it because everything inside cost too much. The Rio lowered its prices, loosened its slots, put in a world-class buffet, and started hosting local events like the Italian Food Festival. Now the place is jumping all the time.

The hotel's theme is a Brazilian carnival, with a rain forest thrown in for good measure. The dealers wear festive shirts and the cocktail waitresses wear hardly anything. The casino is lit with ribbons of neon: bright pinks, reds, teals, and blues. Even the overhead lighting is on the exotic side, with chandeliers shaped like giant nautilus shells.

One of my favorite spots is Búzios, a seafood counter and restaurant overlooking the Rio pool. Named after a sleepy village north of Rio de Janeiro, the food is excellent, especially the bouillabaisse. (Now I'm trying to impress you. How many people do you know who can spell "bouillabaisse"?) Your window view of the pool area sets the mood for a romantic evening. Actually, the pool is more like a lagoon, with a genuine sand beach sloping down to the water's edge and a waterfall splashing in the background.

**Chow down at the Carnival World Buffet.** This is one of the top three buffets in Las Vegas. You've got your choice of Chinese, Japanese, Mexican, Italian, Mongolian barbecue, and American fare—all prepared while you watch. There are also hamburgers, fish and chips, sushi, dessert and salad pavilions, and even a margarita bar (costs extra). This buffet has constantly been voted number one in a yearly Vegas newspaper poll. Don't worry about the lines; this experience is worth the wait.

If you want to take some great pastries back to your room, make a quick stop at Toscano's Deli and Market. The Toscano bakery does a landslide business, with delicious breads, cakes, and specialty items.

**See Danny Gans in the Club Rio.** This topnotch impressionist, with a repertoire of more than 200 different voices, has signed an exclusive contract with the Rio—and his show is one of the best I've ever seen. He does 'em all: Nat King Cole, Natalie Cole, Michael Jackson, Katharine Hepburn, Frank Sinatra, Dean Martin, Clint Eastwood, Jimmy Stewart, Sammy Davis Jr., the Simpsons, even Kermit the frog. As this goes to press, the price is $60 a person, including tax, tip, and two drinks. The show has been voted best in Las Vegas by tourists and locals alike, so make reservations at least two weeks in advance.

**Experience Masquerade Village.** It's Rio, it's Venice, it's Mardi Gras—all fused into one big $200 million hodgepodge of shops, restaurants, and entertainment. Dining spots include the Village Seafood Buffet, Mask, Mama Marie's Cucina, Napa Restaurant & Winery Tasting Room, Bamboleo, and Voodoo Cafe & Lounge (with great views from the top of the new tower).

The highlight of your masquerade escapade is the Masquerade Show in the Sky, an interactive show where onlookers get to put on costumes and join in a themed parade! The 12-minute parades, complete with floats, dancers, musicians, aerialists, and stilt-walkers, take place along a 950-foot track suspended above the casino floor. (That's me standing under the safety net.) Showtimes: Every other hour throughout most of the day and evening.

# Gold Coast

The Gold Coast is across Valley View Boulevard from the Rio, with nice shady covered parking in two enclosed garages. Do me a favor when you go to the Gold Coast. If you see a brown-haired woman with limpid brown eyes playing the slot machines, and if she answers to the name Debbie, tell her to come home! I miss her.

This is one of the most popular local hangouts in town, and with good reason. There's plenty to do, the food is cheap, and the slots actually give you some of your money back. With more than 300,000 members in its slot club, the 2,100 slot and video poker machines at the Gold Coast are always cranking. Join "The Club" and you get a personalized card which you use each time you play. It automatically tabulates points that you can redeem for meals, gifts, and trips. The machine even wishes you a happy birthday if you're playing on your special day.

For recreation, there's the Gold Coast Dance Hall featuring a 15-member orchestra, and the Gold Coast Bowling Center, a 72-lane bowling center on the second floor.

The Gold Coast has a good 24-hour coffee shop and two great restaurants. The Monterey Room features everything from a light snack to a complete meal, with a special Chinese menu after 5 p.m. It's open 24 hours a day and is usually crowded. Come around 4:45 and you won't have to stand in line.

The Cortez Room features prime rib, steak and seafood. Dinners from $8.95 to $21.95. Reservations a must.

The Mediterranean Room serves fresh seafood and Italian specialty dishes. Dinners from $4.95 to $21.95. Again, make reservations.

If you want one of the best hamburgers in Las Vegas, go to Terrible Mike's. The burger comes plain, and you build it the way you want from Terrible Mike's topping bar.

Finally, there's Kate's Korner, with charming decor reminiscent of the old corner drug store. Order a sundae or malted from the soda jerk. This is the only chance you'll ever have to call someone a jerk and get away with it.

Directly across the aisle from Kate's is a great lounge with big screen TV tuned to sporting events. Because it's so crowded, it's hard to get a drink in there, but that makes your trip to the Gold Coast even cheaper!

For a free ride to the Strip from the Gold Coast, take the shuttle. It will drop you at the Barbary Coast, the resort's sister property. The shuttles run continuously, beginning at 9:30 a.m. from the Gold Coast. Last one back from the Barbary Coast is at 12:30 a.m.

**Catch a flick at Gold Coast Twin Theaters**. The Gold Coast has two theaters, and there's always a first-run movie playing. Screenings before 4 p.m. are $4 per person. I like the buttered popcorn; it's only $1 for a big tub. (Of course, they put a lot of salt on it, and their cold drinks are 25 bucks.)

# Orleans

When you think of New Orleans, you think of raucous music, salivatin' food, and earthy entertainment. So when you think of the Orleans Hotel (west of the Strip off Tropicana at Arville), the same images should come to mind. Unfortunately, this hotel—owned by the same group that runs the Gold Coast and Barbary Coast—misses the mark completely.

The only real touch of Cajun Country is the New Orleans-type balconies over the main casino. Another unusual feature is the giant atrium at the front entrance of the 21-story hotel. It's a refreshing change from the marquee-type entrances of other Vegas resorts.

That's about it, though. There's no Louisiana-type food in the whole place, unless you count the crawfish bisque at the Canal Street Grill. What this hotel needs is a neat little outdoor cafe with barbecued crawfish on newspaper, like you get down South, or at least some chickory coffee and 24-hours-a-day git-down Dixieland jazz.

Like the Gold Coast, the Orleans features a state-of-the-art bowling center. Don't forget the Kid's Tyme child care facility, where guests can leave their small fry for up to three and a half hours at $5 per hour per child. (The cages are cleaned regularly.)

What keeps me coming back to the Orleans is the Century Orleans 12, a 12-screen movie complex on the mezzanine level. This is where my wife set the world's record by watching the movie _Titanic_ 278 times. The chairs rock comfortably, there are cup-holders for your drinks, and seating is sloped so that nobody can block your view of the screen. Now if they would just outlaw "Coming Attractions," we would be getting somewhere.

For cocktails, you have your choice of three island bars at the Orleans. There's the Crawfish Bar, with a casual backwoods flavor; the Alligator Bar, where mascot

Al E. Gator hangs out (Al E. Gator, get it?); and the Mardi Gras Bar, with decorative mirrors and Mardi Gras masks that give it a little atmosphere, anyway.

Restaurants at the Orleans include Don Miguel's, Vito's, Courtyard Cafe, French Market Buffet, and my favorite of the bunch: Canal Street Grill, with carved glass doors and a cozy fireplace at the back of the restaurant.

Entertainment hinges around the Branson Theater showroom (based on the one in Missouri), featuring stars like Rich Little, the Smothers Brothers, and Roy Clark. I call it "yesterday's stars at today's prices."

The Orleans must be doing something right, though. They're already spending $40 million enlarging the hotel, and they've only been open since December of 1996. Look for an oyster bar, specialty coffee shop, and gumbo house in the near future.

CASINO SECRET

Take the shuttle from the Orleans to either the Gold Coast or the Barbary Coast. There's no charge.

# Showboat

In 1954, every casino in Las Vegas was either situated downtown or on the Strip. Then a $2 million replica of a Mississippi riverboat opened on Boulder Highway, and locals have been flocking to it ever since. Originally called Desert Showboat Motor-Hotel, the name was promptly changed to Showboat. It's popular for three reasons: bowling, bingo, and bargains.

Showboat was the first resort in town to install a bowling alley and sponsor bowling tournaments. Now Showboat has the largest bowling center in the nation, with 106 lanes and national TV coverage for such events as the PBA Tour and High Rollers. Many Vegas casinos sponsor league play for their employees at Showboat, where I bowled a 300 one night (100 in the first game, 110 in the second game, and 90 in the third game).

There are seats for 1,200 people at Showboat's Bingo Gardens, featuring Bonanza bingo and Super Star bingo. Half a million dollars is up for grabs in Showboat's Super Star bingo tournaments, held quarterly, with $125,000 in cash prizes awarded in each. The entry fee is $170 per person and includes two days of bingo, free meals, and other extras.

For great food bargains, you have a choice of the Showboat Coffee Shop, the Captain's Buffet, and DiNapoli. DiNapoli features good Italian food, with complete dinners starting at $8.95. Showboat's other restaurant, The Plantation Room, is a little on the expensive side, but it's cheaper than flying to Louisiana. Blackened catfish, chicken Pontchartrain, duckling Louisiana, Australian lobster tails, bananas Foster, and Louisiana bread pudding with bourbon sauce are just a few of the Plantation Room's specialties.

Remember, there's a lot to see in Las Vegas. If you're only in town for two or three days, you may not have time to see Showboat. But if you're here for longer than that, it's worth a trip. After all, there's more to Las Vegas than casinos and theme parks. There's casinos and *bowling*.

# Boulder Station

Boulder Highway is also home to Boulder Station, a $100 million gambling resort that opened in 1995. A clone of big sister Palace Station, it's got the same cozy atmosphere and the same great restaurants.

The free-standing sign outside impresses you right away. A hundred and sixty feet high, it features a message center made up of two and a half miles of neon tubing and 66,000 lightbulbs—PLINK—make that, 65,999 lightbulbs.

Focal points inside include stained-glass murals, ceiling fans, hardwood walkways, brick floors, and hand-painted ceilings that combine to give the place a genuine Victorian-age feel. Enough of that, though. Let's eat!

You have a choice of seven fast-food outlets and five full-service restaurants with good down-to-earth prices. Iron Horse Cafe features a Chinese menu in addition to coffee-shop fare; the Broiler for steaks and seafood; Pasta Palace for Italian specialties; Guadalajara Bar & Grille for Mexican food; and "The Feast" Action Buffet.

# Sam's Town

One of the most popular local hangouts in Las Vegas is Sam's Town, on Boulder Highway. It's a great chance to see how the locals play, and there's something here for just about everyone.

• Great restaurants: Diamond Lil's, Willy & Jose's Mexican Cantina, Smokey Joe's Cafe and Market, Mary's Diner, Papamio's Italian Kitchen, Billy Bob's Steak House and Saloon.

• Bowling: 56 lanes with automatic scoring and a complete pro shop.

• RV parking: Two complete parks with 500 spaces each, full hook-ups, swimming pools, laundry facilities, club house, and pet run.

• Final Score Sports bar: Best of its kind with pool tables, pinball, darts, shuffleboard, putting machine, video games, outside sand volleyball, pool, spa, and over 30 TVs so you can watch all your favorite sports action without ever going home again.

• Mystic Falls: A beautiful indoor park with trees, flowers, and cobblestone footpaths, where the temperature is always a perfect 70 degrees. A rustic outside bar overlooks waterfalls and a mountain, and there's a laser light and water show four times daily. The show is free, and will have you screaming for more. (Demi Moore, that is.)

# Sunset Station

The fourth and newest of the Station Casinos projects, Sunset Station—at the intersection of I-215 and Sunset Road—incorporates Spanish culture, Mediterranean architecture, and American slot machines. The outside of Sunset Station is splashed in light peach, with a dozen turrets of gold and blue rising from atop the 20-story hotel. Inside, a sky ceiling, polished tile floors, and a facade of adobe fronts and iron balconies let you feel like you're ambling through a small neighborhood in Spain.

The 600-seat Club Madrid, the outdoor Amphi Theater, a 13-screen (soon to be 24) movie theater, a 7,000-square-foot swimming pool, and an 8,000-square-foot arcade with the latest video games cover the entertainment possibilities.

Wanna drink first? Let's! How about the Gaudí Bar, which is reminiscent of the Art Nouveau period. Everything's kind of curvy in here—and if you don't believe me, try to read that drink menu on the blackboard. Bartender, give us a couple of those Sunset Sunrises, and easy on the vermouth. Wow, you put that one down in a hurry. Okay, let's go to the bar at Rosalita's Cantina. I like the Cuazno Rojo Mezcal, 'cause it's got a worm in it. Eat that worm and you get a free T-shirt. Oh, come on, it's not that bad. I just pretend it's spaghetti. Now over here by the vishing fillage—or rather, fishing village—is the Seville. Best Buddy Marys in Vegas. They make 'em from scratch right in front of you. Tasty, huh? Here, let me help you to your feet, 'cause you gotta see the Ballbatter Boy—err, the Beer Barrel Bell—err, the Bullfighter Bar. It's noisy, but we're only havin' a beer. Oooh, all of a sudden I don't feel so hot. That worm must've given me food poisoning!

Sunset Station offers more than just watering holes: restaurants include the Capri for Italian-style fare in a simulated outdoor piazza; Costa del Sol for seafood and a $7.95 all-you-can-eat salad bar; Rosalita's Mexican Cantina; the Sunset Cafe for 24-hour service; a 50-seat oyster bar with great gumbo and etoufee; and the Feast Around the World, offering five specialty buffets and a dual-sided salad pavilion.

# The Reserve

It's a dark and stormy night. Congo Jack is piloting his two-engine plane over the jungle when one of his engines conks out. Then sparks fly and his other engine quits. "Take over," he says calmly to his co-pilot. "I'll parachute down and get help."

Too late. The plane smashes through the roof of the coffee shop at the Reserve. The co-pilot—a wimp of a chimp who now walks with a limp—crashes into a row of slot machines. Congo Jack falls in love with Monsoon Mary and they live happily ever after in this African-themed casino on the outskirts of Las Vegas.

Well, all right, even though it isn't Caesars Palace, the Reserve is still way ahead of all the other off-Strip casinos when it comes to atmosphere and ingenuity. For starters, the marquee is bordered by massive 40-foot elephant tusks. (They're artificial, okay?) Inside the casino you'll see lush greenery everywhere, and you may even win some of it: one day when I was there, they gave away hundred dollar bills every six minutes, and the promotion-intensive casino plans to keep the giveaways going.

Other nice touches: Hair dryers and coffee pots in all 224 rooms; a sandwich and java joint on the casino floor, three unique watering holes (the Funky Monkey Bar, Monsoon Mary's, Wasimbas), and African scenery everywhere you look. I especially liked the carved-stone animal reliefs, the tribal hieroglyphs on the casino walls, and the hippo pool outside Monsoon Mary's. After drinking a Kilimanjaro Jungle Breeze, I swear I saw a blue hippo in there.

Take your time as you wander through the Reserve. Is that a hidden safari of wild animals in the cloud formations overhead? Is that a black panther lurking in the trees? Is that smoke wafting from Congo Jack's wrecked airplane? The whole thing reminds me of my brother's room when we were growing up. Huminals (half-human, half animal) roam the casino on occasion, along with stilt walkers, musicians, and Tarot card readers.

Another novel approach taken by the Club Reserve slot club is the unique comp service. You can make plans for the evening without leaving your slot machine! Insert your card and punch the service key. You can summon a host by pushing one key, or make your own comped meal reservations by pushing another.

The Reserve boasts four great eateries. The Grand Safari Buffet serves an impressive array of American, Mexican, Chinese, Italian, seafood, and hard-to-find Mongolian barbecue. (Casino workers actually get the same fare in their employee dining room.) Pasta Mombasa specializes in handmade pastas, wood-fired pizzas, and entrees running anywhere from $9.95 to $18.95. Congo Jack's Cafe features California and Chinese-style cuisines. The Reserve's gourmet restaurant is Wildfire Steaks & Seafood, serving mesquite or applewood-fired steaks and other specialties in an atmosphere of rain and thunder. The prices aren't bad, either. Live Maine lobster is only $22.95. If you want it cooked—well, that's another story.

The Reserve has 1,450 slot machines, 26 table games, a sports book, poker room, 300-seat bingo parlor, and a location about as far away from Las Vegas as you can be—and still be in Las Vegas. (Intersection U.S. 515 and Lake Mead Blvd.) If you've got the time and the wheels, it's a definite must-see.

# The Three Northwesteers

First there was the Las Vegas Strip, from the Sahara to Luxor and everything in between. Then there was the Boulder Strip, with the Showboat, Boulder Station, and Sam's Town. Now there's the Rancho Strip, with the Fiesta, Texas Station, and Santa Fe.

**Fiesta** opened in December 1994 at the corner of Rancho Boulevard and Lake Mead Boulevard, and was an immediate success with northwest suburbanites. It bills itself as the "Royal Flush Capital of the World," which gives you an idea how important video poker is to Fiesta's marketing strategy. A neat touch at Fiesta is a drive-up sports-betting window. Just stick your paycheck in the pneumatic tube, and off you go.

Restaurants at Fiesta include the Old San Francisco Steakhouse and Dance Hall, with lots of dark wood, simulated gas lites and a raised dance floor; Garduños, for Mexican food; Cactus Rose Coffee Shop, with great daily specials; Festival Buffet with the biggest barbecue pit this side of Texas (the state, not the casino), and a Mongolian barbecue to rival the Rio's.

The best values for the money are the Festival Buffet and Garduños, which has been voted the best Mexican restaurant in Vegas two years in a row.

Across six lanes of busy Lake Mead Boulevard from Fiesta is **Texas Station**, a sister property of Palace and Boulder Stations. The pumping oil well along Rancho Boulevard lets you know this is longhorn country, and even the sidewalk out front is covered with little Texas-shaped bricks. Texas Station bills itself as the "Royal Flush Capital of the World," which gives you an idea how important video poker is to them, and how competitive they are with arch-rival Fiesta.

Texas Station wasn't nearly as busy as Fiesta the last time I was there, although this casino has a lot going for it. For one thing, there's the 12-theater Texas Cinemas, with a huge snack bar inside. Watch out, though. Popcorn is $3.75, and cold drinks are $2.50.

Restaurants at Texas include San Lorenzo, for Italian food; Laredo Cantina & Cafe, for Mexican; Stockyard Steak & Seafood House; Yellow Rose Cafe, a 24-hour coffee shop; and the Market Street Buffet, which challenges the Rio and Fiesta for top buffet honors.

Two miles north of Texas (the casino, not the state) is **Santa Fe**. The big attractions here are gambling, good food, and ICE SKATING! Yes, Santa Fe is the only casino in Vegas with its own professional ice skating arena (200 by 85 feet). It's available for open skating, private and group lessons, and amateur and semi-professional hockey.

There's also a 60-lane state-of-the-art bowling center, featuring Brunswick's computerized "Bowlervision" system.

Restaurants include Ti Amo, for Italian ($); Pablo's Cafe, 24-hour coffee shop ($); Lone Mountain Buffet ($); Kodiak Lounge Steak House ($$); and Suzette's, for gourmet French cuisine ($$$$$$$$$$$$$$).

# 15
# Near Enough

If you don't want to spend all your time in Las Vegas, several resort areas are near enough to warrant a visit. It'll take you an hour and a half to get to Laughlin, Nevada. Advantages to Laughlin: Cheap meals and rooms at half the Vegas prices. Disadvantages: Hot in the summer, with the country's highest temperature at least 20 days a year, and the fact that everyone else is there for the same reason you are—cheap meals and rooms at half the price.

Of the ten "hot spots" in Laughlin, nine are bunched along the Colorado River. They include founder Don Laughlin's Riverside, Flamingo Hilton, Regency, Edgewater, Colorado Belle, Pioneer, Golden Nugget, Gold River, Harrah's, and Ramada Express (on the other side of Casino Drive).

Laughlin get big crowds from Nevada and Arizona, and that can be another drawback. The town gets pretty crowded. You can save just as much money—in a less jumbled atmosphere—in one of the two areas we are about to visit. I call these areas "fanny pack" country.

# Primm Resorts

In 1950, a young man named Ernest Primm bought 400 acres of land at the Nevada-California state line. "What'll I call it?" he asked a friend.

"Where's it located?"

"Well, it's on the state line."

"State line. Hmm, I dunno."

"How about Bordertown?"

"No, sounds too much like Mexico."

"Well, I could call it Primm."

"No, sounds too—proper. Where'd you say it was?"

"On the state line!"

"State line. Hmm, I dunno."

That's where my very rare copy of the original tape recording ends, but in a way Primm and his friend's conversation was quite prophetic. The land Primm bought became known as State Line, Primm's first casino on the property was called "Bordertown," and State Line's name has been changed to Primm.

Ernest Primm died in 1981, but his son Gary carries on the name and the empire. Chairman of Primadonna Resorts, Primm has built three colorful resorts at Primm: Whiskey Pete's, the Primadonna, and Buffalo Bill's.

You'll have to drive some to get there. It's located 40 miles southwest of Las Vegas on Interstate 15. But if you like a raw frontier setting and cheap entertainment, it's worth the trip. I have friends from California who don't even come to Vegas anymore; they stay at one of the three Primm resorts.

The oldest of the three properties is **Whiskey Pete's**, which started as a two-pump gas station with a dozen slot machines back in the mid-1950s. The proprietor was a crusty old codger named Whiskey Pete, who made his own moonshine in a cave across the road. Today Whiskey Pete's has 777 rooms in an 18-story tower. Whiskey Pete's also has a great restaurant called the Silver Spur

Steak House, where you can get a two-pound T-bone for $12.95. Take a gander at Bonnie and Clyde's "death car," along with the restored gangster car of mobsters Al Capone and Dutch Schultz. There's a complimentary monorail that takes you over to the other Primadonna properties across the highway.

The **Primadonna** has a turn-of-the-century carnival theme, with free rides on an indoor carousel and an outside 100-foot Ferris wheel. At night, the Ferris wheel lights up the lonesome sky with a beautifully animated light show. Other attractions at the Primadonna include an eight-lane regulation bowling alley, an exceptional RV park, and top-name entertainment daily in Gary's Garage.

**Buffalo Bill's** is a Western-theme casino with some big-city innovations. I especially like the Hangman's Bar, where animated cowboys sing and talk under a five-story lighted hanging tree. For the more adventurous, there are two exciting rides at Buffalo Bill's: the water flume logride at "Adventure Canyon," and the "Desperado" roller coaster. Desperado is the tallest and one of the fastest roller coasters in the world, reaching speeds of close to 90 miles per hour. Two friends of mine decided to go up in the Desperado, bragging that they would keep their hands in the air during the entire ride. I learned something that day. People can fly—for a short period of time, anyway.

# Mesquite

Located 80 miles northeast of Las Vegas on Interstate 15, Mesquite is the fastest-growing town in the state. With a population of 6,300, it has a small-town flavor but the big-city excitement of casino gambling. I like Mesquite because it reminds me of how Las Vegas used to be.

The muddy Virgin River winds its way through the region, which is what attracted the first human settlers some 2,000 years ago. These were the Paiute Indians, who believed the river had sacred powers. They also thought the beans from the mesquite trees had sacred powers, and in a way they did. The beans were dried, cooked, then fermented into a potent cocktail. In fact, they say that's how Sitting Bull got his name —after drinking a couple of mesquite martinis, he couldn't stand up.

The Indians were chased away by Spanish explorers, who carved out the old Spanish Trail along the banks of the river. Miners descended on the area in the late 1800s, blasting holes everywhere in their frantic search for gold. Then Mormon farmers moved into the region, raising crops and cattle. This is pretty much how things stayed until the Peppermill Casino was built in 1981. Overnight Mesquite became a secluded hideaway for burned-out Vegas residents and for tourists from nearby Arizona and Utah. In fact, it's almost like a miniature Palm Springs, with plenty of golf courses, palm trees, and sunshine.

**Si Redd's Oasis Resort.** The Peppermill is now owned by Si Redd, the same Si Redd who founded IGT (International Gaming Technology). Redd got his start with a video game called "Pong," which led to his design of the very first video poker machines. His resort is set on more than 1,000 acres, and boasts such amenities as a 500-seat convention area, an RV park, six swimming pools, three spas, and two 18-hole golf courses: the Oasis and the Palms. There's also a petting zoo at his Arvada

Ranch and Gun Club, and a nightly hayride and steak fry. The only drawback is the casino's decor. Accented in reds, blacks, and mirrors, it's almost like being in a carnival fun house.

Have lunch at Peggy Sue's Diner across the parking lot from the casino. There's a different blue plate special each day for $5.45, and old-fashioned shakes and malts served in those fabulous metal containers like you used to get at Walgreen's.

**Virgin River Hotel and Casino**. Just down the road from the Oasis is Virgin River, Mesquite's low-roller joint. Two swimming pools, three jacuzzis, the world's longest bar, two theaters, and a full-hookup RV park are the resort's main attractions.

**Casablanca.** In Mesquite, all roads (well, both of them, anyway) lead to this lush resort, opened in 1995. Once owned by entertainment mogul Merv Griffin (but since sold to the owner of Virgin River across town), you could spend your whole vacation here. Set among 1,000 palm trees with a sparkling lagoon pool and hot mineral spas, it's a dramatic counterpoint to the surrounding desert landscape. Your room charge includes unlimited use of the mineral spa, steam room, and gym.

You can gamble anywhere, and you can eat anywhere, but the spa at Casablanca is something you won't find anywhere else. Begin your experience with a eucalyptus steam and mineral water shower. Afterwards, soak to your heart's content in a warm or hot mineral pool, both which are bordered by rocks and lush vegetation. Then get out the Visa card, because everything else is going to cost you. A 30-minute hand and foot massage is $40, a 1-hour deep-tissue massage is $95, a mudbath body wrap runs from $40 to $60, or you can get a "Watsu," which is a series of exercises in a pool. The pool is private, by the way, so you won't have to worry about someone taking pictures of you for *America's Funniest Home Videos*. Of the three resorts, Casablanca is definitely the one worth seeing. On the minus side, the table games and slots aren't as loose as their Vegas counterparts; the food is mediocre; and the rooms are a long way from the elevators. (It's almost like being on the Bataan death march.) On the plus side, the employees are super-friendly; the pool with slide and waterfalls is one of the best I've seen; and the spa treatments will be remembered for a lifetime. The spa is popular, so make your appointment in advance.

# 16
# Other Attractions

There is much more to do in Las Vegas than drink and gamble and see topless shows. There is also ... hmm. No, wait a minute! There are museums, amusement parks, restaurants, and many scenic wonderlands just over the horizon. Come on, wipe that frown off your face and follow me.

## Debbie Reynolds Hotel

Want to see a real live movie star? Then head for Debbie Reynolds Hotel and Hollywood Movie Museum. Off the Strip on Convention Center Drive, it's one of the most unusual resorts in town. Here the attraction is Debbie herself.

**Take the Hollywood Walk of Fame.** See costumes, props, and other movie memories. Hey, there's Edward G. Robinson's pipe! Hey, there's Edward G. Robinson's humidor! Hey, there's Edward G. Robinson's elevator shoes! Located between the entrance and the showroom, the Walk of Fame is free.

**Tour the Hollywood Movie Museum.** This is the permanent home of a small part of Debbie's private collection, which is valued at over $30 million. Check out costumes worn by Lana Turner, Rita Hayworth, Clark Gable, and Tyrone Power. See Judy Garland's pinafore dress from *Wizard of Oz*, and Elizabeth Taylor's stunning head-dress from *Cleopatra*.

The nice thing about this museum is that you don't just view the exhibits. You also get to sit down and experience them through a high-tech presentation of video and sound. The 35-minute program is followed by a walking tour, where you'll see everything from Marilyn Monroe's subway dress from *The Seven Year Itch* to Barbra Streisand's beaded gown in *Hello Dolly*. Daily tours run every hour on the hour. Admission price: $7.95.

**See *The Debbie Reynolds Show* in the Star Theater.** Debbie, who has been tromping the boards in Vegas since the 1960s, puts on a glittering performance with the Uptown Country Singers. Afterwards, she comes down into the audience, signing autographs and posing for photos. Price: $34.95, including two drinks.

Or for $99.95, you can go on a double-date with Debbie Reynolds and Tab Hunter. Check at the box office for details. Just kidding. Debbie? Tab? I love you guys.

One reminder: If you want to see Debbie perform, call first. Sometimes she's out of town doing other things, like trying to make a living. Her little place in Vegas isn't doing so well, and could close at any time.

# Planet Hollywood

*I, Bruce Lee, will be the highest-paid Oriental superstar in the United States. In return I will give the most exciting performances and render the best quality in my capacity as an actor. Starting in 1970, I will achieve world fame and from then onward until the end of 1980 I will have in my possession $10 million. I will live the way I please and achieve inner harmony and happiness.*

—Signed, Bruce Lee (1969)

This is just one of the priceless pieces of movie memorabilia at Planet Hollywood. Exactly 282 steps inside the Forum Shops at Caesars (I paced it off in my desert boots), it is the trendiest cafe in Vegas. The food is surprisingly good, and if you're not sure what to order, the waitress will help you.

We ordered blackened shrimp for an appetizer, chicken Caesar pizza on thin crust, Thai shrimp pasta, ebony and ivory brownie for dessert, and cappucino with Italian biscotti as a nice finale.

I gave the meal a "D." (Delicious.)

Aside from the food, "the Planet," as people in the know call it, has a flashy splashy atmosphere that brings in the customers in droves. I can't use any fancy adjectives to describe Planet Hollywood, because better writers than I have already used them all, and I don't want to be accused of plagiarizing someone else's stuff. Eric La Brecque wrote the best line ever. In his magazine article, *Living On Planet Hollywood*, he said, "We are what we eat. Increasingly, however, we are also what we dream." Apparently, Eric had just downed a couple of Terminators in the Planet Hollywood bar. (A Terminator is a mixture of vodka, rum, gin, Cointreau, kahlua, beer, and cranberry juice.) Hasta la vista, baby.

Planet Hollywood is a variation on an old theme: nostalgia. The Hard Rock Cafe did it first with music, now Planet Hollywood has done it with movies. In fact, four of the principal shareholders of the Planet chain are movie stars Bruce Willis, Demi Moore, Sylvester Stallone, and Arnold Schwarzenegger. I guess you could call it a four-star restaurant.

I wander around the place in awe, because I'm a movie buff like everyone else. I've done the Universal tour and I've seen the autographed footprints of the stars at Grauman's Chinese Theater. But most of that is from another era, and Planet Hollywood is now.

The Vegas branch of Planet Hollywood is a two-story affair, and each floor is broken up into themed sections. There's the Hollywood Hills, with movie star cut-outs; the Sci Fi Room, a mockup of the Starship Enterprise control board flashing overhead; the Monster Bar, where Pinhead, Freddy Krueger, and the Animatronic Zombie double-dare you to order another round of drinks; Bedrock, complete with Flintstone movie memorabilia; the Sly Room, named for you know who; and the Main Room, right in the center of it all.

Within eyeball distance of any table is something sure to twang your memory strings: Elvis Presley's high school yearbook. (His major was shop.) You'll also see the motorcycle and side car from *Indiana Jones' Last Crusade*; Laurence Olivier's uniform from *The Prince And The Showgirl*; John Wayne's outfit from *The Cowboy*; Natalie Wood's overcoat from *Gypsy*; the moon buggy from *Diamonds Are Forever*; Warren Beatty's robe from *Bugsy*; Yul Brynner's costume from *The King And I*; James Dean's shirt and jeans from *Giant*. And suspended over the Main Room is the miniature train used in *Under Siege 2: The Dark Territory*.

The place is mobbed on weekends (between 10,000 and 12,000 people stream inside), so go during the week when it isn't quite as noisy. Pick up a T-shirt ($17) or a reversible leather jacket ($325) so everybody knows you've been there. Wave goodbye to the friendly staff when you leave. They are trained from infancy to love you like family.

It's a nice way to spend a couple of hours, gorging yourself silly and then walking it off while you take in all the memorabilia. As a spokesman for Planet Hollywood told me, "It's a place where adults can be adults, or where they can be kids again." By the way, Bruce Lee attained his goal of making $10 million, and he did achieve world fame, but he died in 1973.

# Dive!

Another popular theme restaurant in Las Vegas is Dive! Located in front of the Fashion Show Mall on the Strip, Dive! is a unique concept in dining and underwater entertainment. At Dive! you can eat a sub while you're *in* a sub.

Talk about atmosphere! My wife and I took some friends to Dive! for lunch. They're from a little town in Texas where everything is barbecued, and for some reason people who like barbecue are hard to please. Well, they raved about Dive! It's the first place they want to go every time they're in Vegas. On the other hand, a friend of mine from Chicago got seasick. Me? I enjoyed it so much that I'm actually living there now. Those aren't dead fish draped over the bathysphere. Those are my socks.

The exterior of Dive! is moored at one end by the yellow and purple nose of a life-size submarine, protruding into a 30-foot water wall. At the other end is a 35-foot lighthouse that welcomes guests with a flashing beacon. Between the sub's nose and the lighthouse is the body of the restaurant, painted gunmetal gray and accented by porthole-shaped bubble windows. You enter the restaurant through an open hatch, of course, but one of the nicer touches is the battery of periscopes stationed nearby. You can zoom in on the Strip until the hostess calls your name, or you can zoom in on a blonde until your wife calls you names. You also might want to check out the sub's safety features. Do those giant band-aids really keep the ship from leaking? And does the piping overhead resemble a musical instrument, or is that just your imagination?

Owned by a very rich group of businessmen, including Vegas tycoon Steve Wynn and Hollywood producer Steven Spielberg, this is one of the coolest spots you'll find in Vegas on a hot afternoon. Let me set the scene for you.

It's exactly two o'clock. Suddenly lights flash, overhead pipes blast with steam, a foghorn alarm sounds from the sonar control bridge. Orders to clear the deck are heard, and then through your porthole you see millions of bubbles as you sink deeper and deeper into the depths of a calm underwater world.

From the video wall in the main hull (and on 48 additional monitors throughout the restaurant), you go on a film adventure that brings you face-to-face with sea turtles, sharks, barracuda, whales, manta rays, Jacques Cousteau—and then you drift past the breathing beauty of coral gardens into the middle of Jellyfish Lake! Millions of undulating jellyfish surround you, but the fearless sub plunges on, through underwater caves and racing currents, until finally you're staring at the sunken hulk of the great Titanic.

Well, I guess I mentioned everything. Oh, wait a minute! The *food*!

You have a choice of almost two dozen different submarine sandwiches, as well as light pastas, gourmet pizzas called "Portholes," and daily specials from the galley. My favorites were the fried carrot-chip appetizer, the homemade chocolate-chip-cookie sundae, and the strawberry cruise, a blend of fresh strawberries and vanilla ice cream topped with whipped cream.

The original menu was in development for more than a year, with each of the partners trying out 100 different creations. The ones upon which they agreed now grace the menu. The only problem is trying to get Steve Wynn back down to 180 pounds.

# Country Star

Question: What do Wynonna Judd, Vince Gill, and Reba McEntire have in common?

Answer: They all wear cowboy clothes, they all sing cowboy songs, and they all helped found the Country Star American Music Grill food chain—which now has a Las Vegas address on the Strip north of the Monte Carlo. The outside of the restaurant features a mockup of a 60-foot jukebox, which tells you right away that this isn't your regular run-of-the-mill barbecue joint.

Inside, you're treated to interactive kiosks that allow you to "communicate" with your favorite country stars on video. Or you can just wander around and check out the country music memorabilia, including the Patsy Cline exhibit and the Elvis room. I especially liked Merle Haggard's grade-school diploma, Hank Williams Jr.'s AA certificate, Johnny Cash's pill box, and some photographs taken at a party celebrating Brenda Lee's 85th birthday.

But what you're really here for is the food, and I just happen to have a menu in my barbecue-stained fingers. Skip the appetizers (cheese toast, chili cheese fries, and the like) and go directly to the headliners. These include chicken-fried steak ($12.95), the cowboy steak ($21.95), and the big barbecue feast for two or more, which includes all kinds of hickory-smoked meats ($16.95 a person). Best thing on the menu for the price is the hickory pork sandwich served on a hamburger bun for $8.95. Reminds me of Texas back in the '50s—except that the same sandwich cost 75¢.

# Wet 'n Wild

This resort doesn't have a casino. It doesn't have a nice restaurant. It doesn't even have any rooms. In fact, this place is all wet! It's Wet 'n Wild, a sparkling water park on the north end of the Las Vegas Strip. What a great way to beat the heat on a hot summer day. That is, if you don't mind being in the same water with 5,000 other people. Keep your hands where I can see 'em, pal!

There's plenty to do, so bring some sunscreen and plan on staying awhile. (This is a very popular park, so come around mid-afternoon when lines are at a minimum.)

**The Black Hole.** The thrills of a flume ride with the drama of darkness.

**Raging Rapids.** First you bob along in an inner tube, then suddenly you plunge into a pool of water 40 feet below.

**Willy Willy.** Inner tube again, only this time you're zipping clockwise.

**Banzai Boggan.** A water rollercoaster in a two-passenger sled.

**Blue Niagara.** A six-story drop through 300 feet of blue inner space.

**Bomb Bay.** The ultimate free-fall, 76 feet straight down in two seconds.

**Der Stuka.** Scariest of the bunch, where you dive-bomb down a 100-foot runway into a pool of water. Excuse me, but has anyone seen my bathing suit?

**Whitewater Slideways.** Two water slides, one enclosed, that shoot you down a twisting 50-foot flume into a splash pool.

**Flash Flood Hydra-Maniac.** Spiral through a 1,000-gallon-a-minute burst of water.

**Surf Lagoon.** This giant pool (with 500,000 gallons of water) offers the excitement of real ocean-sized waves without the fear of sharks and other creatures.

**Lazy River.** My favorite of them all, where you float around the park on a giant inner tube at about one mile an hour. The only way you can get injured is by climbing out of the inner tube incorrectly, which is how I hurt my back.

There's also a children's water playground, snack bars throughout the park, and plenty of neat shady spots to get out of the sun. Admission: $21.95 for adults, half price for seniors over 55, and $15.95 for kids under 10. (Prices may be higher by the time you read this; they seem to go up every year.) Open from May through September. Operating hours vary, depending upon the month.

# Harley Davidson Cafe

Attention, all bikers and road mamas. Now you've got your own little piece of hog heaven. It's the Harley Davidson Cafe, and like it's really hard to find. Just look for a seven-ton hog sticking out of a building 28 feet in the air on the Strip at Harmon Avenue. What? No, not a real hog, man, but a *hawg*—a Harley Davidson.

For food, you've got your meatloaf, your chicken pot pie, your Sloppy Joe's, your K.C.-style barbecue, your Harley Hog pork sandwiches. What? No, not a hawg, man, but a hog—a real hog. And they're all under nine bucks. If you really want to "pig out," try the fajitas ($10.95) or the sirloin steak dinner ($16.95).

After all that chow, you might need to change your T-shirt from a medium to an extra large, and that's easy, too. Just hit the retail shop, where they've got all kinds of Harley gear. Then scope out the Captain America motorcycle from the movie *Easy Rider*. It's the same bike on which sat the stoned butts of Peter Fonda and Jack Nicholson.

Oh, and one more thing before you go. Try the slot machines at the Harley Davidson Cafe. If you hit the jackpot, you win a hawg! No, not a hog, man, but a hawg— a Harley Davidson.

Now hit the road.

# Official All Star Cafe

Have you seen that 100-foot Coca-Cola bottle on the Strip next to the MGM Grand? That's where you'll find the Official All Star Cafe, a three-level restaurant that's probably more popular for its sports memorabilia than for its meals. I mean, the food's okay, but you can get a hamburger anywhere. Where else, though, can you get a close-up peek at Elvis Presley's bowling trophy, or Babe Ruth's baseball bat, or the Lakers' chair from the Forum on which sat the butt of Jack Nicholson? You might even see Tiger Woods' golf socks. (There's a hole in one.)

Six sports stars are partners with owner Robert Earl in the All Star Cafe, and each one has a dish on the menu. There's Andre Agassi's spaghetti pomodoro, Wayne Gretzky's T-bone steak, Ken Griffey's chicken-fried chicken, Joe Montana's ravioli, Shaquille O'Neal's smoked turkey sandwich, and Monica Seles' chicken Caesar salad.

Adding to the atmosphere is a center-court scoreboard with up-to-the-minute scores, videos of great moments in sports, and dining booths shaped like big baseball mitts. There's also the Andre Agassi Room, where you can almost smell Andre's tennis shoes from the 1994 U.S. Open while you enjoy your dinner. If that doesn't whet your appetite, I don't know what will.

The Official All Star Cafe is one of five tenants at the Showcase Mall, a $94 million entertainment center with five levels and an 11-story parking garage. You might as well see everything else while you're at the Showcase, including:

- United Artists Showcase 8 Theatre, the only first-run movie theater on the Las Vegas Strip.
- GameWorks, a combination theme park and game arena put together by Sega Enterprises and Universal Studios.

• The World of Coca-Cola/Everything Coca-Cola, with lots of Coca-Cola nostalgia and a spectacular soda fountain.
• M&M's World/Ethel M Chocolates, featuring four levels of retail candy stores and dessert bars.

COMING SOON? The Pepto Bismol/Tums Emporium — with stomach pumping right on the premises.

# Liberace Museum

A welcome diversion from the fast pace of Vegas is the Liberace Museum, located at 1775 East Tropicana, about a mile east of the Strip. Here you will get an intimate glimpse into the world of "Mr. Showmanship." Although Liberace died in 1987, his music and legend live on, and you can almost feel his presence in this elegant museum.

The museum houses Liberace's 1962 Rolls Royce Phantom, completely mirrored in tiny mosaic tiles; his 1934 Mercedes Excalibur, covered in Austrian rhinestones; and his red, white, and blue Rolls Royce convertible. You also get to gaze at his fabulous wardrobe gallery; check out the fox fur coat with jeweled lining that he wore during his last tour.

Stroll through a re-creation of the master bedroom from his Cloisters estate in Palm Springs. Then in the museum library, see the collection of press clippings and rare photographs that chronicle his life. There's much more. His stage jewelry, rare crystal and china, piano-shaped wristwatch, the Chickering grand piano once owned by George Gershwin, and Liberace's favorite item: the Chopin piano, actually played by Chopin at Versailles. Admission: $6.50 for adults, $2 for children under 12.

(For a good cheap Italian meal, have an early dinner at Carluccio's. This family-style multi-roomed restaurant is located in the Liberace estate's Tivoli Gardens directly behind the museum. There's one of Liberace's pianos in the main bar, which is also piano-themed.)

# Lake Mead

We're going to take some side trips now, all within an hour or so of Las Vegas. If you want more information on any of the following scenic areas, pick up free brochures and maps at one of the five Clark County visitor centers. The one in Las Vegas is located on Paradise Road at the Convention Center. The visitor centers offer a free information service on hotel or motel reservations or Las Vegas entertainment, and will even mail you an information packet. So keep this number handy: 702-892-7575. Now on to Lake Mead.

Lake Mead is the largest man-made lake in the United States. It has 822 miles of shoreline, 291 square miles of water surface, 9.9 million visitors a year, and 130 bathrooms. (In other words, you ain't going where no man has never gone before.)

Americans who want to watch where their tax dollars go should take a look at the new fee-collection guard shacks under construction at the Lake Mead entrances. Then take a guess as to how much the government allocated for each shack: (A) $90 (B) $900 (C) $9,000 (D) $90,000 (E) $900,000.

Well, of course it's E. With Washington involved, what else could it be?

Located 25 miles southeast of Las Vegas, Lake Mead National Recreation Area offers fishing, boating, camping, picnicking, hiking, swimming, waterskiing, diving, and plenty of scenic drives. It also offers flash floods, abandoned mines, blistering heat, unsafe drinking water, poor roads, fire ants, rattlesnakes, scorpions, Gila monsters, and plenty of intoxicated fellow travelers.

Of historical note, nomadic Indian tribes settled this area in prehistoric times, subsisting on bighorn sheep and smaller game, on yucca and pinion pine nuts, and on Big Gulps from a primitive 7-11 store. When the waters of

Lake Mead recede during dry periods, you can see the tops of old buildings poking out of the water in spots. Certified divers will take you down to explore the once-flourishing town of St. Thomas, founded in the closing months of the Civil War and buried under the waters of Lake Mead after Hoover Dam was completed.

A good place to start your visit to Lake Mead is at the Alan Bible Visitor Center, four miles northeast of Boulder City on U.S. 93. The park staff can help plan your itinerary, and maybe show you how to make splints for broken bones out of old Popsicle sticks. You can also get maps and information on park activities and services. Nearby is an outdoor botanical garden that displays some of the area's interesting desert trees, shrubs, and cactuses. Or is it cacti? Well, they can tell you.

For an unusual vacation, rent a houseboat and live on the water. During peak season, June 15-September 15, a houseboat that sleeps six will cost you $950 for a weekend. Off-season it's $650. What I want to know is how much does it cost just to take a picture of one?

If you would rather let someone else do all the work, take a cruise on the paddlewheeler *Desert Princess*. Leave from the Lake Mead Marina on a dinner cruise ($43), a snack cruise ($14.50), or a weekend breakfast cruise ($21). For congressmen on fact-finding tours, the prices are a little higher: $47,000 for a dinner cruise, $26,000 for a snack cruise, and $34,500 for a weekend breakfast cruise.

You can also take a raft trip down the Colorado that begins at the foot of Hoover Dam and ends 12 miles down the river. Or do as my wife and I did, and go on a canoe trip down the same stretch. It took us three days and introduced us to many interesting facets of nature—including some wild animals that don't even have names yet, and a guide named Art who was actually able to sleep on the ground.

Note: Avoid Lake Mead during summer holidays,

such as Memorial Day or July 4th. As many as 250,000 people flock there on holiday weekends—to get away from it all.

# Hoover Dam

Before Hoover Dam was built, the area around Las Vegas was a great big desert. Come to think about it, it's still a great big desert. But at least we've got water now, which gives us something to argue about with Arizona and California.

Hoover Dam was opened by President Franklin Roosevelt in 1936, five years after construction began. Seventy stories high, the massive concrete dam turned the muddy and sometimes violent Colorado River into the still clear waters of Lake Mead. More than 5,000 men worked day and night to build the dam between the deep and rugged walls of Black Canyon, and today it's listed as one of the seven modern wonders of the world. Roosevelt called the dam "an engineering victory," then went on to say:

"Today I consider myself the luckiest man on the face of the earth." No, wait a minute, that was Lou Gehrig, who spoke immediately after the president.

You can reach the dam by driving southeast from Las Vegas to Boulder City, some 24 miles away. Boulder City, the only city in Nevada where gambling is not allowed, was created by the government to house the people who worked on the dam. Worth seeing in Boulder City is the stately Boulder Dam Hotel. Built in 1933 to host visiting dignitaries including President Roosevelt, the hotel is best remembered as the place where Clark Gable and Carole Lombard spent their honeymoon.

Actually, Hoover Dam was originally called Boulder Dam. The name was changed in 1947 to honor former president Herbert Hoover. When Hoover learned of this great honor, he said, "Today I consider myself the luckiest man on the face of the earth." A lawsuit was immediately filed against him by the family of Lou Gehrig.

When you get to the dam site, check out the new Hoover Dam Visitor Center, which took 13 years to build

at a cost of $120 million, $88 million of that in cost over-
runs. Worse, it's financed over 50 years, so with interest
the visitor center will cost us a total of $435 million be-
fore it's paid for. But in return we get two theaters, two
restrooms, an exhibition gallery, an overlook, and four
elevators.

Walking tours of the dam run every 10 minutes during the day, and you get to descend 428 feet. You also
get to ascend 428 feet, so bring some walking shoes. Tours
are $5.

Frankly, though, I think Hoover Dam is a big disap-
pointment. There's not one slot machine or blackjack table
in the whole place!

# Red Rock Canyon

Go west on Charleston Boulevard as far as you can go and you'll eventually wind up at Red Rock Canyon, one of the area's prettiest and rawest examples of Mother Nature throwing a tantrum. Actually, it's only 17 miles so you can easily drive it in 45 minutes. If you go by bicycle, it will take you six hours. If you walk, it will take you all day. If you hitchhike, it'll take you about three weeks.

The 130-mile National Conservation Area that includes Red Rock Canyon is resplendent with tall canyon walls splashed in color, sandstone bluffs, secluded canyons, underwater springs that bubble out of the ground, and a picturesque 13-mile loop that winds through the most scenic part of the canyon.

It's a recreational paradise, with sightseeing, picnicking, hiking, rock climbing, horseback riding, jogging, photography, and bike touring. A friend of ours talked my wife and me into riding the 13-mile loop on bicycles. We haven't spoken to him since.

But let's backtrack and start our trip from scratch. As you enter the Red Rock Conservation Area, you will see a turnoff to the right. This is Calico Basin, a small settlement of homes scattered beneath Red Rock Canyon. There's a nice picnic area (to the left of the homes) called Red Spring. Great spot to eat and enjoy the view.

The next turnoff is the Red Rock Canyon National Conservation Area. Start this portion of your trip by visiting the Visitor Center, open daily from 8:30 a.m. to 4:30 p.m. Behind the Visitor Center is the 13-mile scenic loop that takes you past Calico View, Calico Vista, White Rock, the Willow Springs picnic area, Lost Creek Canyon, Ice Box Canyon, and Pine Creek Canyon. Darn it, I forgot to bring my binoculars, but if you squint real hard you might make out some tiny dots on the sides of those canyons. Those are people. A lot of rock-climbers try scaling these jagged canyon walls, which keeps the "Flight For Life" helicopters busy.

We're back on the main highway now, and the next turnoff to the right takes us to Spring Mountain Ranch. Since we're not in a big hurry, let's stop there. While you try to get out of the back seat of my Hyundai, let me give you a little history on this place. You see that spring-fed stream that runs through the ranch? There are actually 52 springs in this area, and that's what attracted settlers back in the 1830s, when a campsite was first established here.

It also attracted outlaws, who made a living by pouncing on unsuspecting caravans that were trying to take a shortcut off the old Spanish Trail. They were chased off by mountain man Bill Williams and a band of Ute Indians, and afterwards the site was known as the "old Bill Williams ranch." Then a former Army sergeant and his partner filed a claim on the property, naming it the Sand Stone Ranch. They raised cattle and went broke. A family friend paid off their debts and took over the ranch. He raised chinchillas and went broke.

In 1944, the ranch was leased to Chester Lauck, who played Lum on the old "Lum and Abner" radio show. He raised hell and went broke. No, actually Lauck finally bought the property and built the main ranch house, calling it the "Bar Nothing Ranch." In 1955, Lauck sold the ranch to Vera Krupp, the wife of a German munitions industrialist. She added a swimming pool and another wing to the main house, including a secret bedroom.

Mrs. Krupp sold the ranch to Howard Hughes in 1967, but it is said that Hughes only stayed one night and suffered a horrible accident there. He got his beard caught in his toenails. When Hughes died, the Summa Corporation sold the property to two businessmen. Their great American dream was to level the ranch and build condos on the land. This brought such an outcry from the public that the Nevada State Parks Division stepped into the picture. They bought it with the public's money, and now they're charging the public to see it! Well, I see you finally got out of the car. Come on, let's walk over to the Ranch House Visitor Center.

Oh heck, the darn thing's closed. I guess I forgot to mention that the Visitor Center is only open from 12 p.m. to 4 p.m. on weekdays, 10 a.m. to 4 p.m. on weekends and holidays. Maybe next time you're here we can take a walking tour, and even have lunch at the picnic area under the shade of an old oak grove. Or we could go to an evening concert, and sit out under the stars. Be sure to pour your beer into a 7-Up can, though. Alcoholic beverages are not permitted. Okay, back to the car.

Now I want to warn you about the wild burros you'll see up ahead on the side of the road. You didn't just give one of them an apple, did you? Well, don't do it again. It makes them congregate on the roadway, that's why, and a lot of them have been hit by cars because of thoughtless people like you! The way it was explained to me by the park people was that you should pick a safe place to stop, pull completely off the roadway, and observe the burros from a distance. They are wild animals, and can be dangerous. Count your fingers. See! I told you.

One more turnoff, and then we'll get you to the emergency room. The next right takes us to the entrance of Bonnie Springs Ranch, originally a way station built in 1843 for travelers crossing the Mojave Desert on their way to Knott's Berry Farm. It was discovered by a young Mexican scout in 1829, which must have been news to the Paiute Indians. They'd been living there since the 1500s.

Bonnie Springs has a great little wood-clapped restaurant and bar overlooking a shady pool of water. Don't wear a tie, or it'll wind up with thousands of others hanging from the bar rafters. You can watch ducks float lazily on the water or tour the Bonnie Springs Petting Zoo and see all kinds of cuddly creatures—some of whom could use a bath in that water right this minute.

Across a rickety bridge is the town of Old Nevada, a faithful recreation of an 1800s' frontier town. There are shops, mock gunfights in the street, silent movies at the Bijou, and a miniature train that snakes between the parking lot and the box office. There's also an admission charge of $6.50 for adults and $4 for kids. I recommend going back to the bar instead and making an offer on that gorgeous purple-and-orange polka dot tie hanging from the rafters.

# Mount Charleston

For a cool getaway from the heat, spend a day up on the mountain. Mount Charleston, that is. Rent a car if you don't have one, and drive 45 miles northwest on the Tonopah Highway (Hwy. 95). On the way, you'll see a turnoff to Floyd R. Lamb State Park. It's a nice park with plenty of ponds, trees, picnic tables, ducks and peacocks. Unfortunately, there's a shooting range right next to the park, which kind of spoils things. It's almost like having a picnic at Normandy during the D-Day invasion. So let's skip the park, and head directly for Mount Charleston.

Take a left at Kyle Canyon Road (Hwy. 157) and up you go. First you'll see the desert in all its primitive beauty. Then slowly, pine trees begin to replace cactus as you enter the Toiyabe National Forest. Suddenly, there you are on Mount Charleston, 11,000 feet high, which is about as high as you can get in the state of Nevada without breaking the law. Take a sweater, because the temperature will be around 20 degrees cooler.

Halfway up the mountain is the Mount Charleston Hotel, where you can spend the night with all the comforts of home. Other services on the mountain include the Mount Charleston Lodge (great hot toddies), and Mount Charleston Resort, where you can rent a log cabin or go horseback riding. The resort also offers hayrides in the summer and sleigh rides in the winter.

But the nicest thing about Mount Charleston is the cool peaceful solitude, with plenty of secluded campsites and picnic areas. One of my favorite memories was the night I was chopping down a 1,000-year-old bristlecone pine tree for firewood. No, I'm kidding; I was just sitting under one. Then suddenly, by the light of the moon, a gray wolf came ambling down the roadway. He perked his ears as he walked past me, but didn't hurry his gait at all. It was as though he was thinking, "Oh, he's harmless." As he disappeared, the wind began to blow, starting out as a gentle wisp of a breeze, gaining momentum as it surged through the trees, finally reaching a crescendo that almost sounded like the ocean on a stormy night. Okay, maybe that doesn't do much for you, but after fighting the crowds in a casino all week, this was a great moment for me.

There are two overnight campgrounds on your way to Charleston Peak: Kyle Canyon Campground and Fletcher View. There's also the Cathedral Rock Picnic Area. At the end of the road is Mount Charleston Resort and the quaint Mount Charleston Lodge. On your way back down, take a left at Highway 158. You'll start to climb again as you go past Hilltop Campground, Mahogany Grove Picnic Area, and Foxtail Canyon Picnic Area. These are okay, but you can do better.

Take a left at Highway 156. Now you're on your way to Lee Canyon, a skier's Eden in the winter, but a summer paradise as well. On your right is the Old Mill Picnic Area, and then the two best campgrounds on the mountain: McWilliams and Dolomite. The trees here are tall and stately, and you've got the whole place practically to yourself because everyone else wheeled into the first campground they saw.

Oh, by the way, don't leave just yet. Go up the mountain a few hundred yards to the Lee Canyon Ski Area. In the winter, there are three double chair lifts in operation, ten ski trails, a snowboarding area, and a ski lodge with full rental equipment, food, and drink. The highway department is good about keeping the roads cleared of snow drifts, but check first. If they tell you that you need chains, then do as I do. Go to Valley of Fire instead.

# Valley of Fire

Take Interstate 15 northeast for 55 miles and you'll see the turnoff to Valley of Fire State Park. Nevada's first state park, Valley of Fire is famous for its wild rock formations that litter an almost moon-like landscape. The sandstone formations are streaked with reds and oranges, and were formed from great drifting sand dunes during the age of the dinosaurs. Over the millennia, the dunes hardened, then erosion set in, and the result is some of the most majestic scenery in Nevada.

The Indians discovered it in 300 B.C. and used it as a sort of vacation getaway. They couldn't live there because there wasn't enough water, so they only came for a few days at a time. They would do a little hunting, maybe have a religious ceremony, carve some pictures on the rocks, and then go home. That doesn't sound like my idea of a vacation, but everyone to their own tastes.

The best time to visit Valley of Fire is spring or fall. During the summer, temperatures can get as high as 120 degrees. Wear comfortable shoes, because you'll have to hike to the more interesting spots. Here's what to look for.

**The Beehives**. Sandstone formations shaped like—beehives!

**Petrified Logs**. Logs that washed into this area from ancient forests 225 million years ago.

**Atlatl Rock**. Site of an Indian petroglyph depicting the atlatl, which was a notched stick used to add speed and distance to a spear. The question you'll ask yourself is how the graffiti artists got up the 80-foot sheer rock face to carve on it. Today, there's a 100-step staircase leading there, which is the highest such staircase in the state.

**Petroglyph Canyon**. Take a self-guided half-mile walk through a sandy canyon, and see prehistoric Indian drawings on the canyon walls. Go past this, and you'll come to: Mouse's Tank a natural basin in the rock where water collects after infrequent rainfalls. It's called Mouse's Tank because back in the 1890s a renegade Indian named Mouse used to bushwhack prospectors when they'd come up here for water. If my parents named me Mouse, I would probably do the same thing.

**Seven Sisters**. Red rock formations right off the road.

**Elephant Rock**. Probably the most famous formation in the park.

**Rainbow Vista**. Panoramic view of some colorful sandstone.

There's also a trail you can take from Rainbow Vista that goes through Fire Canyon to a unique geological site called Silica Dome. Round-trip, it's a three-mile hike, so don't try it unless you're under 20. Instead, take the new Scenic Spur Road and drive three miles. You'll see some of the Valley's most interesting formations, such as Arch Rock and Piano Rock.

Be on the lookout for wildlife. They're mostly nocturnal, but you may see a coyote, kit fox, spotted skunk, black-tailed jackrabbit, antelope ground squirrel, roadrunner, or desert tortoise. There are rattlesnakes in the area, too, but don't panic if you see one. Simply remain motionless until the snake slithers away. If the snake doesn't leave, sing a Wayne Newton song. That usually works.

On your way out of the park, have a picnic at the Cabins, a group of cabins made of natural sandstone in the 1930s as a haven for passing travelers.

When you leave Valley of Fire, you can either drive back to Las Vegas the way you came, or take Highway 169 a couple of miles northeast to the Lost City Museum at Overton. Indian artifacts are on display, as well as reconstructions of Anasazi Indian dwellings dating back nine centuries. I didn't think it was really that special. It looks like the neighborhood where I grew up.

# 17
# Bonus Secrets

The idea behind this book was that the casino secrets alone would cover the cost of it. Just to make sure you do get your money's worth, I'm ending this book by turning it into another fabulous Las Vegas resort.

All right, the fountains are going, there are fireworks in the sky, here come the topless showgirls (EVERYONE BACK TO THEIR SEATS, PLEASE), and now on the computerized marquee we present even more casino secrets!

**CASINO SECRET:** If you'd like to get married in Las Vegas, shop around. You'll find that there's a wedding chapel to suit every taste—and every wallet. Choose from Chapel of the Bells (in the "heart" of the Las Vegas Strip), Silver Bell Wedding Chapel ("We Pay for Your Marriage License"), Little Church of the West (more celebrities married here than any other place in the world), and Little White Chapel. This one has a drive-up wedding window. You don't even have to get off your motorcycle.

If you can't tear yourself away from the casino long enough to tie the knot, then get married at the Stratosphere (800 feet above the city), Treasure Island Wedding Chapel, Riviera Wedding Chapel, Flamingo Hilton Garden Chapel, We've Only Just Begun Wedding Chapel inside the Imperial Palace, Circus Circus Chapel of the

Fountains, Central Park Wedding Chapel at the MGM Grand, Monte Carlo Wedding Chapel, Tropicana Island Wedding Chapel, or Celebration Wedding Chapel at Bally's.

Is it a spur of the moment thing? Then get married at the Clark County Courthouse downtown. A couple once asked me where they could get married right away. I told them about the County Courthouse, which was only a 10-minute cab drive away. "That's good," the man answered. "Because we've got to be back at work by 3 o'clock."

**CASINO SECRET:** Make sure you bring your camera, and film as well. A roll of Kodak film, 24 exposures, generally costs about $4.50 at the grocery store. Buy it in a Las Vegas hotel gift shop and pay about $5.20. Bring your snacks, too. A 45¢ candy bar will cost 80¢ in the gift shop, and the same kind of price mark-up applies to everything else.

When I questioned a gift-shop manager about this, he shrugged. "When you pay more rent," he said, "you have to charge higher prices." I was so choked up I almost gave him a dollar.

**CASINO SECRET:** Always cash in your chips before leaving the casino. Chips from one casino are not negotiable in another. This is to guard against counterfeiting, and to keep casinos from having to make time-consuming and expensive chip runs to other hotels.

On the other hand, metal $1 tokens can usually be used at any casino in town. Just drop one in a slot machine down the street, and see what happens.

**CASINO SECRET:** For the cheapest meals in town, try the casino buffets. Every hotel has one. Some are good; some are great. You'll pay more for dinner than you will for breakfast or lunch, but there's a better selection of food that usually includes ham, turkey, and prime rib sliced off the bone. Breakfast buffets generally run around $5, lunch is about a dollar more, and dinner costs anywhere from $6.95 to $12.95.

Circus Circus has one of the cheapest buffets in town. But by the time you get to the front of the line for the dinner buffet, it'll probably be time for breakfast again.

Which ones should you try? The Rio's Carnival World Buffet has received numerous accolades for being Las Vegas' best. Other exceptional buffets include the Festival Buffet at the Fiesta, the Market Street Buffet at Texas Station, the Palatium Buffet at Caesars Palace, the Island Buffet at the Tropicana, the Paradise Garden Buffet at the Flamingo Hilton, the Mirage Buffet, and The Buffet at the Golden Nugget. The Buffet is also one of The most expensive.

The weekend in Las Vegas means champagne brunches. Some are cheap, some cost as much as a used car. The $10 Sunday brunch at Santa Fe's Ti Amo features bloody Marys at one bar and coffee and liqueurs at another. A jazz trio serenades you in the background.

One of the best is the Sunday Sterling Brunch at Bally's ($50 per person). It's a lot of money, I know, but I only go there on special occasions: like when I hit the lottery. The $50 includes fresh orange juice, oysters on the half shell, chilled shrimp, Beluga caviar, made-to-order omelets, filet mignon stuffed with mushrooms, lobster tail, and flaming desserts. Keep repeating to yourself as you pay the bill, "It wasn't a meal, it was an experience. It wasn't a meal, it was an experience. . ."

**CASINO SECRET:** Thumb through the Las Vegas Yellow Pages and you'll see almost 100 pages of "Adult Entertainers." These ads offer anything your heart desires: dirty deeds done dirt cheap, your fantasy is my reality, nasty college girls, tonight will be your night, two at a time. All of these come-ons were culled right from the phone book. Beware! All you'll get is a little dance and a big bill. Prostitution is illegal in Clark County, so don't fall for it. You're better off reading *Playboy* for $5...which is about 1/60th of what it will cost you for an "adult entertainer."

**CASINO SECRET:** Need a band aid, wheelchair, oxygen? For first aid or any other emergency treatment, contact hotel security. (Tip: Bring aspirin from home. Casinos will not dispense any kind of pain reliever, including aspirin.) Need a hair dryer, space heater, crib, fan, or refrigerator in your room? Just call room service. And speaking of rooms, there are lots of valuables in them that are yours for the taking. (Hey, put that television back!) Check the bathroom. Those little containers of shampoo, face soap, hair conditioner, and skin cream cost as much as $10 a set in the gift shop. You get 'em free.

**CASINO SECRET:** You're inside a casino. Where's a good place to eat? Where are the shops? What is it that really sets this resort apart from all the others? There's one way to find out in a hurry, and that's to ask an employee. The employees know more about the hotel than anyone else, and they'll be happy to share this information with you.

**CASINO SECRET:** The best things in life are free, or so the old song goes. In Las Vegas, that can still be the case. For instance, just take a leisurely stroll in any direction on the Strip, and you're bound to be entertained without it costing you a cent. People-watching is a great pastime. Heck, I just like to read their T-shirts. Or you can just stand there and marvel at the buildings. These are the biggest hotels in the world, all lined up in a row. Enjoy the grandeur, and think of Las Vegas as the country's last true frontier city. It really is, you know. And where else can you see a 30-story pyramid next door to a castle, with a six-story lion right across the street? A friend of mine said it best: "Think of Las Vegas as the World's Fair and each casino as one of the pavilions."

**CASINO SECRET:** Make a free phone call! Just pick up a house phone in most casinos and call any other casino in town absolutely free. You don't even have to know the number.

Keep in mind that Las Vegas is a constantly changing city. By the time you read this, some of the resort attractions will have probably changed and prices might be higher than those quoted. Remember too that you're here to unwind and have fun. Don't let the town or the people intimidate you.

I only wish that you could have seen the real Las Vegas, but that era of intimacy and personal attention is long gone. Today each Vegas resort is a factory, but the one thing that hasn't changed is the dream. Something is going to happen any minute, something that just might change your life.

Good luck.